Ethical Idealism

ETHICAL IDEALISM

An Inquiry into the Nature and Function of Ideals

NICHOLAS RESCHER

University of California Press
Berkeley · Los Angeles · London

University of California Press
Berkeley and Los Angeles, California

University of California Press, Ltd.
London, England

Library of Congress Cataloging-in-Publication Data
Rescher, Nicholas.
Ethical idealism.

Includes index.
1. Ethics. 2. Ideals (Philosophy) I. Title.
BJ1012.R43 1987 170 86-6946
ISBN 0-520-05696-5 (alk. paper)

Printed in the United States of America
1 2 3 4 5 6 7 8 9

For Jerry Massey
in cordial friendship

Contents

Preface

Metaphysical idealism stresses the importance of value in the world's scheme of things. Ethical idealism—the theme of the present volume—stresses the importance of value in the sphere of human action. The present book is a companion piece on the side of ethical idealism to various earlier publications of mine that have dealt with metaphysical idealism.

The studies that constitute this essay were drafted in Pittsburgh during the 1983–84 academic year and were completed in Oxford during the uncharacteristically warm summer of 1984. In polishing these essays during the subsequent academic year, I have profited from the helpful comments of James Allis. And I am very grateful to Mrs. Christina Masucci for her help in guiding the manuscript through numerous revisions in the word processor.

Pittsburgh PA
September 1985

Introduction

This small book examines the nature and function of ideals. It endeavors to show that they play a positive and productive role in human affairs, despite the fact that there is always something unrealistic and unachievable about them. The central thesis is that ideals are important, notwithstanding their impracticability, because of their capacity to guide thought and action in beneficial directions.

The first chapter maintains that it is not irrational to aim at the unachievable. Setting an "impossible," in principle unrealizable, goal can be perfectly sensible when one does so because of a recognition that various positive benefits would result from its adoption.

Chapter II argues that an obligation is not automatically abrogated by the impossibility of its accomplishment. The principle "*ought* implies *can*" makes perfectly good sense—but only in ideal-order morality, not in the imperfect conditions of the real world. The rules of ethical conduct are by nature dedicated to the never fully achievable task of making a place for an ideal in the hostile environment of the world's realities.

The third chapter criticizes the widespread conception that rationality should be construed in terms of maximization. For maximization presupposes mensuration, and human goods and goals are just too diversified to be commensurable. Some combinations of the desirable are simply unattainable in this, the real world. And just this provides the basis for *ideals.*

Chapter IV maintains that in principle it can make perfectly good practical sense to proceed in a spirit of optimism even where our prospects are small or indeed nil; an optimistic attitude can be appropriate even in circumstances where a favorable outcome is implausible and unlikely. For optimism can in principle be defended not only on the (dubious) factual claim that it represents a correct predictive account of the tendency of the world's affairs, but also on the grounds that it has positive effects on our doings and dealings in a difficult world.

The fifth chapter maintains the power and efficacy of ideals. Like the equator and the prime meridian, they cannot be encountered actualized in physical embodiment on the world's stage. But like these other idealizations, they constitute an eminently useful and productive instrumentality of thought and action.

Finally, the sixth and last chapter argues that ideals, even though not realized or even realizable in this mundane dispensation, can nevertheless serve to structure our actions and give meaning and guidance to our endeavors. Man can and ought to be regarded as a creature who aspires to something "larger than life"—who looks beyond what *can* be to what *should* be, aspiring beyond particular goals to governing values and ideals. Their practical utility as instruments for the realization of our ends means that the cultivation of ideals can be perfectly rational, notwithstanding their unrealistic and visionary character.

Throughout, the book is concerned to support an accommodation between the real and the ideal by maintaining the usefulness of ideals and idealizations as instruments for charting our way amid the difficult realities of this world. The governing line of thought is straightforward. Man is a rational agent who often does and generally should orient his actions by an intelligent recourse to values. And ideals, unrealistic though they are, can nevertheless provide important guideposts towards the optimization of values.

Something significant is at stake with ideals. Recent trends in ethical theory indicate that the study of virtues and vices must be based on a proper appreciation of the fundamental role of moral ideals and aspirations.[1] Ideals are important both because of their critical guiding role at the level of personal decision making and because of their utility in rendering the behavior of rational agents amenable to explanatory understanding.

Many virtues and aspirations are best regarded in the light of ideals. In particular, ideals help us to understand and validate acts of supererogation. Take courage, for example. Acts of courage generally extend beyond the call of duty. They are best understood in terms of a commitment to a certain ideal of moral excellence. Neither alone nor in combination can an ethic of requirement do the whole job. Whether our interest is in understanding or in guiding human behavior, there is work that can be accomplished properly only by an ethic of ideals.

We thus obtain an instrumental defense of the importance and validity of ideals. A central theme of these deliberations is that ideals can serve as useful instruments for practice and that the validation of ideals lies in their utility—in their capacity to facilitate the realization of the practical ends to which our values bind us. Paradoxically, the book develops a justificatory rationale for the ideal in terms of its utility for human praxis.

The reader who seeks doctrinal substance rather than general principles here—who looks to the book for ideological advocacy rather than a theoretical analysis—is destined to go away disappointed. The discussion focuses on the general issue of the nature and justification of ideals, asking such questions as what

[1] See, for example, Nicholas Rescher, *Unselfishness* (Pittsburgh, 1975); David Heyd, *Supererogation* (Cambridge, England, 1982); and C. H. Sommers, ed., *Vice and Virtue in Everyday Life* (New York, 1985).

ideals are, what sorts of work they do, and how they can be appraised and validated. It abjures ideology: it does not present a concrete philosophy of life and does not seek to recommend the adoption of certain particular ideals. As is common in philosophical deliberations, it views its subject from a somewhat Olympian perspective. Its aim is to help the reader to think more clearly about his own ideals rather than to proselytize him by recommending those ideals that the author himself happens to find congenial.

I

Lost Causes

On the Rationality of Pursuing Unattainable Goals

Synopsis

(1) Can it make good rational sense for someone to adopt an unattainable goal, pursuing an objective whose nonrealization is a foregone conclusion, (2) and which is even recognized by the agent to be such? (3) In principle, it can indeed make sense—when that impossible goal is linked to others that actually are achievable. (4) Automatically denying such an unattainable goal the status of a "real" goal is unwarranted. (5) Even when a goal is seen as unattainable, its adoption may still be sensible if its pursuit conduces toward realizing the good at issue. Aiming too high may well be an advantageous policy. (6) While adopting an impossible goal is often foolish, there are nevertheless some cases in which its rational justification can plausibly be maintained. (7) The rationality of impossible goals can be defended, by decision-theoretic means, among others. (8) To be sure, this defense of impossible goals hinges their validity on their utility; it is essentially pragmatic.

1. *The Problem of Lost Causes*

Can it make sense for someone to pursue an unattainable goal, or is the adoption of such a lost cause automatically irrational? Are unattainable objectives not inherently inappropriate from the rational point of view? Consider the argument schema:

- *X* is a rational agent.
- *X* adopts and pursues the goal *G*.

Therefore: *X* believes the attainment of goal *G* to be possible for him.

Does not this reasoning represent a clearly valid inference because rational agents must—given that hypothesis of rationality—set themselves only goals they deem achievable? After all, rational action is a matter of the *intelligent* pursuit of *appropriate* goals. Is pursuit of the unattainable not simply a version of "attempting to do the impossible" and as such necessarily contrary to reason? These questions pose issues that are of interest both in themselves and because their consideration serves to illuminate the nature of rationality.

The present discussion will maintain that, contrary to received opinion, it is actually *not* irrational to aim at the unachievable. It will be argued that the adoption and pursuit of impossible goals can make perfectly good rational sense in suitable circumstances.

We shall not be concerned here with what *lawyers* speak of as "attempting the impossible"—with the man who, intending to steal an umbrella, inadvertently takes his own, mistakenly believing it to be another's; or the would-be assassin who, intent on murder but unaware that a more efficient colleague had been in action before him, pumps a bullet into a corpse.[1] Certain acts

[1] See H. L. A. Hart, "Attempting the Impossible," in his *Essays in Jurisprudence and Philosophy* (Oxford, 1983), pp. 367–91.

are indeed *legally* impossible: one cannot steal one's own possessions or murder someone who is dead. But in such cases we are not really dealing with actions that are impossible for the agent under some even slightly more general description. The thief is unquestionably capable of stealing umbrellas, the assassin of killing people. The particular act under consideration is disqualified from coming under this description by what might be characterized as "a mere technicality."

A "lost cause" in the sense of the present concerns is a commitment to an objective whose nonrealization is a foregone conclusion of a more deep-rooted kind. The entire venture is foredoomed to failure—not just by some fluke or quirk of fate, but for reasons of fundamental principle.

The attempts of Longomontanus (d. 1647) to square the circle and of the Quaker delegation of 1938 to dissuade the Nazis from persecuting the Jews are certainly cases in point. But these are lost causes in an especially strong sense—it would have been impossible for anybody or almost anybody to have attained these objectives. It is not in *this* overpowering way that my endeavoring to run a five-minute mile is a lost cause (after all, many people can do it). The uneven distribution of ability, power, and resources in this world means that something impossible for some might prove a picnic for others. And so, there are various modes of infeasibility: being impossible for anybody, for X as such, or for X in the particular conditions in which he temporarily finds himself. All such cases fall within the purview of present relevance.

A lost cause, then, is a human project whose inevitable failure lies deep and firmly rooted in the condition of things: an undertaking that is hopeless from the very outset.

But is not the adoption of such goals ipso facto irrational?

2. *The Cognitive Aspect*

The pursuit of a goal is a matter of adopting a policy or program of action, and the rationality of actions turns pivotally on matters of cognition. It may in fact be that Melinda's medical condition is hopeless, and that the physician who is trying to save her is engaged in an impossible task. But if he does not *know* that, there is nothing irrational about his energetic pursuit of the goal of saving Melinda's life. There is nothing inherently irrational about adopting and implementing an unattainable goal whose unattainability the agent at issue neither *does* nor—in the prevailing circumstances—even *can* recognize.

The question of the rationality of somebody's action thus depends crucially on how things look from the standpoint of this agent's information. In particular, *if realization of a desired goal is possible to the very best of the agent's responsibly formed knowledge and belief*, then its pursuit by him can be altogether rational, even if it should in actual fact be something whose attainment by him is really impossible.

After all, if one had to determine that realization of a goal is actually possible before its adoption would be rationally warranted, then we would be in very sad straits indeed. In numerous and important cases it is simply not feasible for us to assess the attainability of a goal short of its adoption and pursuit. Given the capabilities of the other competitors, it may actually be impossible for me to win the competition, but in general I cannot *know* that until I actually make the attempt. It may, in the circumstances, be impossible for Tom to win Mary's hand, but that is not something he can determine before adopting that goal and attempting its realization. In life we seldom know in advance of "having a try" and actually pursuing a goal whether or not its attainment is possible for us. If rationality required settling this matter in advance, the path of reason would be even more arduous than it actually is.

Moreover, even if somebody actually *thinks* attainment of a certain goal to be impossible for him, it may still be perfectly rational to adopt the goal. For while the agent does indeed believe in that goal's unachievability, he may nevertheless not be *quite* sure and *altogether* certain. If the only way to safety lies in a leap across a chasm that I do not think I can accomplish, I may nevertheless be well advised in some circumstances to make it my goal—and can do so without any compromise of rationality. Often, indeed, deeming a goal unrealizable is actually just a matter of deluding ourselves so as to create an excuse for not even trying, thus averting the risk of failure. We do well generally to take facile judgments about the inaccessibility of goals with a grain of salt.

But what of the less pliable case, when I do not just think or believe that I cannot attain the goal, but when I actually *know* at the outset that I cannot attain it? Can I rationally adopt this goal even then?

Surprisingly, there are conditions under which even this can be justified. Let us consider them.

3. *Rationale No. 1: Other Fish to Fry*

One situation in which it seems perfectly sensible and rational to adopt and pursue an impossible goal is when doing so is demanded by *other* goals that actually are attainable. In such a case the impossible goal is so intimately *linked* to other, potentially realizable goals that, in the circumstances, their effective cultivation requires that it too be adopted and pursued.

Consider, for example, the commander who sets out to win a hopeless battle, because doing so is demanded by his conscience—or, less admirably, by his wish to impress his superiors. In such cases the agent also has other fish to fry: the impossible goal at issue is indissolubly bound up with other objectives that are, in principle, perfectly attainable, but whose effective cultivation in those particular circumstances demands the pursuit of that impossible goal as well. It is integrally part and parcel of a wider complex of goals, some or most of which are indeed attainable.

The proper appreciation of cases of this sort hinges on distinguishing two sorts of benefits that are at issue with the adoption and implementation of a goal. First, there are the *direct* benefits that would result from its attainment. Second, there are the *oblique* (or *indirect* or "*side*") benefits that will—or can reasonably be expected to—accrue also from its adoption and pursuit, quite apart from the issue of its own attainment. This distinction is crucial for present concerns precisely because the pursuit of an impossible goal can very possibly have substantial oblique benefits when this goal is an integral part of a whole, which has other parts that are in fact realizable.

The person who quixotically sets out to pursue a recognizedly impossible goal is not *necessarily* being an idiot. He may perfectly well realize that he will not succeed in building a perfectly efficient engine or making a perfectly accurate measurement. But he may also be (reasonably) persuaded that certain valued results can best be achieved through making a valiant though foredoomed effort at pursuing that unattainable objective. Pursuing a recognized chimera may well—in some cases—predictably embark us on a great journey of self-discovery and personal development that is not otherwise available. Tilting at those windmills may give meaning to an otherwise empty and pointless existence.

In the presence of such associated side benefits, people can fight for lost causes in a perfectly reasonable way by casting a side glance at such oblique benefits as appealing to "the judgment of history," "making a statement," and staying on good terms with one's conscience. If those associated benefits are a part of what motivates someone in pursuing an unachievable goal, this pursuit will not actually be irrational (even though it may well *look* silly to the skeptical bystander).

4. *A Defensive Countermove: Feasible Ersatz Goals*

There is, to be sure, the defensive move of endeavoring to save the thesis that "Impossible goals are irrational" in such circumstances by maintaining that the impossible goal at issue is not real at all but only a nominal or ostensible goal. The agent's *real* goal is the realization of its fully feasible associates. The strategy is to upgrade those associated side benefits into the main event, elevating them into being "the *real* reason" for the agent's actions.

But this move has its difficulties. Consider again the commander facing a hopeless battle. Using the present argument, one would say: "The commander is not really trying to win the battle—he just wants to acquit himself respectably by putting up a good fight. His *real* goal is 'putting up a respectable fight'." But in fact this just is not so. That less ambitious goal probably would neither satisfy his conscience nor suitably impress his superiors were they to become aware of it. The substitute "real goal" just does not seem to do the job—neither from the angle of psychological description of the agent's state of mind nor from that of a purposive explanation of his actions. The switch to a feasible ersatz goal simply fails to do justice to the agent's intentions and endeavors. Our commander *really is trying* to win that hopeless battle. His fight for a lost cause is fought with good heart in an appeal over the head of a certain defeat for the admiration of posterity—a feasible coordinate goal that, important though it is, does not displace that basic infeasible one.

The problematic nature of this recourse to a distinction between "real" and "ostensible" goals becomes manifest by pressing the question: "Just where is it that we are to locate the difference between a 'real' and an 'ostensible' goal?" Is a "real" goal (in the sense of the present distinction) to be one that the agent *confidently expects* to attain? Surely not! People standardly pursue all sorts of goals in whose ultimate attainment they do not have much confidence. Various politicians who declare their candidacy for the U.S. presidency and bend their every effort toward achieving this goal usually do not quite *expect* to achieve it. In their heart of hearts they may see their chances as relatively small. Yet they are prepared to commit themselves and put all their every hope and energy to the realization of this objective. Their goal is evidently the presidency as such, not some weasly second cousin, like "having a try at the presidency." Clearly, the "reality" of a goal cannot sensibly be made to turn on the agent's estimates of the *probability* of its realization.

One might, to be sure, play it safer and say that the goal's "reality" in this present sense is going to turn on the agent's view of the *possibility* of its realization. Goals whose attainment one deems impossible are thereby automatically rendered merely ostensible goals. But this move is clearly ad hoc—a matter of gerrymandering the concept of a "goal" to save the thesis that a rational agent cannot "really" set impossible goals for himself. From the agent's point of view—and from that of the observer as well—*there just is no further operative difference* between pursuing a goal whose probability of realization is seen as minuscule and pursuing a goal whose probability is seen as nil. That supposedly "merely purported" goal is actually "as real as can be" for our agent because (*ex hypothesi*) he does *everything* that someone who did not recognize the goal's infeasibility would do (and would sensibly do) toward its realization. It is not just that he *says* that that is his goal, but that he believes and acts it, doing all that anyone—even someone who sees it as wholly attainable—can do in its direction.

5. Rationale No. 2: Enhancing Achievement by Aiming Too High

Let us now turn to another, rather different sort of rationalization of impossible goals.

Even when a goal is recognized to be unattainable as such, its adoption may, nevertheless, qualify as perfectly sensible when its pursuit conduces effectively—perhaps even optimally—toward realizing the good at whose promotion this goal is oriented. For example, perhaps only by striving for a *perfect* performance is the performer (a violin soloist, say, or a figure skater) able to do as well as he can (flawed though that performance will inevitably be). The actor who tries to make *every* member of the audience feel anger or irritation may well recognize that he is embarked on an impossible task because some minds are bound to be wandering. And yet the actor may be psychologically so geared that he can give the role his very best only by attempting this impossible objective of reaching "the *whole* house."

Of course one could here once more try to salvage the thesis by transmuting that lesser objective ("performing at maximal effectiveness") into the agent's *real* goal, dismissing the agent's infeasible putative goal as inappropriate. Thus in that previous example, one might take the line: "That actor is not really trying to reach *every* member of the audience, that is just his *ostensible* goal; his *real* goal is simply reaching *as many as possible.*" But the previous critique applies once again. The contemplated goal-substitution just cannot be justified by anything actually on the stage of the agent's views and intentions. Dismissal of the agent's avowed (albeit infeasible) goal is the external fiat of a theorist seeking to protect a pet thesis.

The New Testament enjoins: "Be ye perfect!" Expediency countermands: "No, just be as good as you can." Conscience demands: "Try to win that hopeless battle!" Expediency countermands: "No, just do what you can toward putting up a good fight." We have here once more that tempting reduction of impossible goals through a possibilistic scaling-down—the automatic change from the impossible goal of "realizing *G*" to its miniaturization as "bringing it about that one has done what one can toward realizing *G*." But clearly, if it is applied *only* to unrealizable goals, then this scaling-down tactic at issue is simply ad hoc and question-begging. And if the approach is universalized, grave problems arise. For the automatic "translation" from a particular goal of the form "realize *G*" to one of the form "bring it about that you've done all you can toward realizing *G*" makes for an obvious falsification of the realities of purposive deliberation.[2] The lover's goal is clearly to marry the girl, not just to have done all he can in this direction. The avaricious man wants to have the money, not just the cold comfort of feeling that he has done all he can to get it.

Substituting that less ambitious ersatz objective as the agent's

[2] To avert a potential infinite regress, one must construe "bringing it about that you've done all you can to bring it about that you've done all you can to realize *G*" as tantamount to simply "bringing it about that you've done all you can to realize *G*."

real aim, having it stand as surrogate for the unattainable goal that the agent (*ex hypothesi*) actually has in view, remains an arbitrary and unjustifiable step if taken in the absence of any further specific justification—simply to save a congenial thesis from difficulty. And one searches in vain for any *independent* justification of this maneuver.

It is worthwhile to consider this second sort of justification of impossible goals from another angle of approach.

The police chief of a large city may adopt the goal of abolishing corruption from his force. The safety engineer of a large factory may set himself the goal of eliminating industrial accidents in the plant. Each of them may realize perfectly well that the goals they are setting are unattainable—that failure to realize them in full is a foregone conclusion. And yet they may feel, quite justifiedly, that only by setting themselves those impossible goals can they realize optimal results.

To compromise by adopting a lesser, "more realistic" goal is in many circumstances to settle for a lesser *realization* as well. For we recognize that in many cases something like the following relationship obtains:

Goal at Which We Aim	*Expectable Achievement*
to do perfectly	90% perfect
to do as well as I possibly can	80% "
to make a really strong effort	50% "
to achieve 50%	40% "

Perhaps only if I set out to remember the name of *every* person to whom I am introduced will I succeed in remembering the name of even half of them. Only by actually trying to get *all* those calculations right will I be able to have 90 percent of them correct. There seems good reason to believe that the human condition is such that there is an inevitable gap between aspiration and achievement. A sort of friction or entropy operates to prevent our achieving so ample a result as we aim at. The "inefficiency" will of course vary from context to context—in some spheres we may have a 90 percent realization rate, in others merely 50 percent, and so on. But the principle remains: often it is only by trying for too much that one can get enough.

But if you actually realize that even by "going for it all" you are only going to get 90 percent, then is not getting 90 percent your *real*—actual as opposed to merely *ostensible*—goal when you try for totality in such a case? Not at all. By hypothesis, it is only by trying to get *all* those calculations right that you will succeed with 90 percent of them. If you "slack off" and try for 90 percent, you will in fact get only 70 percent. Your aiming for that impossible result of 100 percent represents a perfectly authentic (and by no means unreasonable) goal, even though you realize that your achievement will fall short of it.

Once this situation is accepted, and it is acknowledged that there is in general a gap between goal or aspiration on the one hand, and result or achievement on the other, then we are led to recognize that attaining an optimal result may in fact require adopting an unrealizable goal. When this happens, it is not—contrary to all appearances—*irrational* to adopt such a goal.

Such situations of "overcommitment" are an inverted variant of "weakness of will" cases. With weakness of will, we believe that we *should* do something, but cannot quite get ourselves to try to do it; with overcommitment, we believe that we *cannot* do something, but we cannot quite hold ourselves back from trying to do it anyway.

Consider the difference between the presumably impossible goal of (1) "getting all the *X*'s there are," and its more "realistic," scaled-down cousin, (2) "getting as many *X*'s as I possibly can." Do these not effectively come to the same thing? After all, one might argue, there is nothing *more* one possibly can do toward realizing (1) than to proceed to realize (2).

But there is in fact a substantial difference. For one thing, I can adopt (2) as a goal in cases where I reject (1) outright: I might well go to the beach with a view to "collecting as many shells as I possibly can" but yet have no intention or aspiration toward "collecting all the shells there actually are on that beach." Moreover, I might adopt (1) in cases where I would reject (2) as a totally inadequate formulation of my aim. The propagandistic pamphleteer wants actually "to persuade *all* his readers," not just "to convince as many readers as he can manage to persuade." Accordingly, one must recognize the inappropriateness of simply "translating" a totalistic goal as per (1) into a maximalistic revision as per (2).

To be sure, the important difference at issue here will not be discernible at the *behavioral* level. Observing someone in process of frantically collecting *X*'s does not inform us whether he is endeavoring to get as many *X*'s as he possibly can or whether he is trying to get all the *X*'s there are. But this simply shows that here, as elsewhere, we must secure more than observationally accessible behavioral information to get a firm cognitive grip on people's goals.

6. *Can Rationality Survive in the Presence of Unrealizability?*

Setting oneself *certain* impossible goals is obviously foolish, hopeless, and crazy: to leap across the Grand Canyon, to drink all the water in Lake Superior, or to have one's cake and eat it too. But what makes the adoption of *these* impossible goals irrational is not simply their impossibility as such but their lack of redeeming features—of associated side benefits whose value could sensibly be taken to outweigh the problems inherent in the pursuit of these particular goals.

To be sure, unrealistic goals are frequently counterproductive. No doubt, all people in some circumstances—and perhaps some people in all circumstances—may find unrealizable demands intimidating rather than encouraging. In some instances, perfectionism may deter people from making any effort at all. When examining the validity of impossible goals, one must take into account the nature of the situation and the makeup of the individual; it is a matter of balancing advantages and disadvantages.

The fact remains, however, that there will undoubtedly be some situations and circumstances in which "aiming too high" is determinably the best way to achieve optimal results. The natural scientist's pursuit of definitive truth and cognitive adequacy ("the truth, the whole truth, and nothing but the truth"), the conscientious agent's pursuit of moral perfection, or the benevolent statesman's pursuit of peace among nations and goodwill among men, all represent putatively unattainable objectives. But they are none the less justifiable—indeed meritorious and noble—for all that.

The scientific case is especially interesting. As Karl Popper and C. S. Peirce before him have insisted, we must acknowledge the infeasibility of attaining the final and definitive truth in matters of scientific theorizing—in particular at the level of theoretical physics. And this seems perfectly correct. From all indications we shall never be able to bring science to a definitive conclusion; the scientific world-picture seems destined to crumble in the wake of the scientific revolutions of the future, regardless of what the "present" at issue may be. It seems to be the inevitable destiny of physics that its practitioners in every generation see the theories of an earlier era as mistaken, full of errors of omission—and of commission as well. In all probability the physicists of the year 3000 will deem our physics no more correct than we ourselves deem that of 100 years ago—and the same ultimate destiny doubtless awaits their own views in turn.

The upshot, we are sometimes told, is that a fallibilist must necessarily abandon the traditional view that the pursuit of truth is a cardinal aim of science, seeing that the "definitive truth" lies beyond the reach of realizability. But this, of course, is stuff and nonsense. The pursuit of truth is rendered no more absurd by the impossibility of its full attainment than is the pursuit of longevity or morality.

But what can possibly be the point of pursuing a goal one

cannot attain? The present analysis indicates that there may well be a perfectly good point, that there are crucial ways in which this impossible goal can be redeemed by its productive features:

(1) The pursuit of definitive scientific truth is an integral component of a wider goal structure (including satisfactory prediction, explanation, and control) whose elements indeed are achievable. It conduces toward a vast spectrum of associated cognitive side benefits of eminent desirability: helpful answers to questions, useful predictions, etc.

(2) There is good reason to think that it maximizes achievement. To turn from truth to "plausible opinion" or "communal conformity" or the like just would not (and perhaps could not) provide a comparably powerful stimulus to spurring greater effort, maintaining high standards, etc.

Both of these modes of justification militate in support of the impossible aim at issue in the scientist's pursuit of the "definitive truth" about the workings of nature.

The long and short of it is that while adopting an impossible goal is often foolish, there are nevertheless some cases—and even important cases—where it is the course of wisdom rather than folly.

Consider the following contention: "If an agent deems a goal impossible, then he is not in a position to count *anything* he does as a means toward actually achieving that goal. How, then, can he (and we) possibly claim that this item represents the goal of his activities?" Can someone actually adopt and pursue a goal whose realization he deems impossible? Clearly *you* can have a goal that *I* think to be unrealizable. But can *I* myself adopt such a goal?

Though this question may *seem* pivotal for our discussion, it actually is not. The real question is not *can someone do this?* For that is a matter of course—people can do endlessly silly things. The pertinent question is whether someone can do it *reasonably* (rationally, sensibly, justifiably). Here we confront the argument: "Once that goal is seen as impossible, a rational agent surely cannot set out to achieve *it,* though doubtless there might be things connected with it that could appropriately constitute goals for him." Plausible though it may seem, this objection just does not hold water. For someone to have a goal, it just is not a rational requisite for him to think that it is something that *will*—or even *can*—be realized.

The adoption of a recognizedly unattainable goal would be automatically irrational only if adopting a goal necessarily committed one (on penalty of self-contradiction) to seeing it as attainable. And this just is not so. Cognitive dissonance need not be engendered by adopting an impossible goal, because the inference from "*X* (reasonably) adopts goal *G*" to "*X* deems the attainment of *G* possible for himself" just does not hold. What is impossible about an "impossible goal" in the presently operative sense is not that it cannot be *pursued,* but only that (*ex hypothesi*) it cannot be *achieved*—that it represents an outcome that lies outside the range of possible realization.

Yet how can something be a sensible person's goal if he sees it as unattainable? The answer is that it suffices for him to see this as something devoutly to be wished for and to bend his thoughts and efforts toward its realization. He need not see its attainment as a realistic prospect—or indeed even as a genuine possibility. When a rationally competent agent adopts an impossible goal, there need not be self-delusion—he need not fool himself into thinking that it is after all realizable. All he need do is to recognize, however dimly, that its adoption and pursuit are conditions of such value as to offset the circumstance of its unachievability. Even as, with the so-called Preface Paradox, the author can, not implausibly, believe every sentence he writes to be true, and yet concurrently recognize that there are falsehoods somewhere along the line, so in the case of those mathematical calculations I can, not implausibly, set out to get each and every one right and yet recognize my goal of getting *all* of them right as simply impossible. There is nothing irrational—let alone impossible—about this.

In adopting a recognizedly impossible goal, if I were committed to the claim that "I *can* actually realize it," then its adoption would indeed be incompatible with that realization of unattainability. But in (rationally) adopting such a goal I am in fact saying no more than "I am well advised to *try* to realize it—that is, to work toward its realization." Nothing in such a stance is actually *inconsistent* with a recognition of unrealizability.

Can one sensibly take the line that it would be reasonable for someone to adopt and pursue a goal even though he deems it unrealizable? Yes, of course one can. One can do so by endeavoring to convince him that taking this step would yield various good results wholly apart from the matter of the goal's attainability.

"But if I do really believe that achieving the goal is impossible, then I just cannot get myself to adopt it." Too bad! That is *your* problem—a problem in the psychology of self-management. From the angle of present concerns, the issue is quite a different one: not whether people can get themselves to adopt a recognizably impossible goal, but whether if and when they do so it can ever be said that they have acted *rationally* in this regard. (If someone concedes that it would be rational for him to do something, but cannot get himself to do it, he falls within the range of deliberations regarding weakness of will, and this lies outside the scope of our present concerns, which are oriented at practical rationality as such.)

7. *A Decision-Theoretic Perspective*

A schematic picture of the way in which goals operate is as follows:

$$\text{adopt the goal} \rightarrow \text{pursue the goal} \rightarrow \begin{cases} \text{succeed?} \\ \text{fail?} \end{cases}$$

Accordingly, the adoption of a goal will have two sorts of costs and benefits: the *immediate* ones associated with its pursuit as such, and the *ultimate* ones associated with the eventual outcome. The former, pursuit-connected (immediate) costs and benefits are effectively certain; the latter, outcome-connected (ultimate) costs and benefits are, in general, *contingent* through their dependence on how matters finally eventuate. In rational deliberation about the adoption of goals we are, of course, entitled (indeed *required*) to take both sorts of costs and benefits into account.

The salient aspect of impossible goals is of course that the ultimate outcome is *not* contingent. Failure in goal attainment is (by hypothesis) a foregone conclusion. And the potential benefits of success are automatically denied us. All the same, the benefits of pursuit may simply outweigh the negativities of (inevitable) failure. Indeed, just this transpires (so we have argued) with the sorts of cases that have concerned us here. And when it does happen—and the benefit of pursuit outweighs the negativity of nonrealization—then the adoption of an impossible goal is not necessarily irrational.

But does the pursuit of an unattainable goal not automatically entail certain negativities, such as inevitable failure, frustration, and dissatisfaction, that vitiate the whole process? The appropriate answer must grant that this is indeed bound to happen to some extent. But the real issue is one of relative weight, and the matter turns on the question: Do these bad effects of failure *outweigh* the presumed good effects of adopting and pursuing that goal? And here the answer is possibly yes, though by no means necessarily so. As we have seen, there will certainly be cases where the balance of benefit favors the adoption of an unachievable goal.

Consider the following situation of a choice between two alternative goals, G_1 (an "impossible" goal) and G_2 (a "possible" one), as per Display 1. Standard decision theory sees the rational resolution of this choice situation in terms of a comparison of expectations:

$$\mathrm{E}(G_1) = (0 \times X) + (1 \times Y) = Y$$
$$\mathrm{E}(G_2) = (p \times U) + ((1 - p) \times V) = \mathrm{V} + (\mathrm{p} \times (\mathrm{U} - \mathrm{V}))$$
$$\mathrm{E}(\text{not-}G_1 \text{ and not-}G_2) = Z, \text{ where } Z < Y$$

Display 1 THE CHOICE BETWEEN AN IMPOSSIBLE GOAL G_1 AND A POSSIBLE GOAL G_2

Adopt and pursue G_1.

success: G_1 realized (probability O)—payoff X

failure: G_1 not realized (probability 1)—payoff Y

Adopt and pursue G_2.

success: G_2 realized (probability p)—payoff U

failure: G_2 not realized (probability $1 - p$)—payoff V

Adopt neither G_1 *nor* G_2.

result (probability 1): Z (which, we shall assume, is $< Y$)

Nothing in the nature of things blocks the prospect that the first quantity should predominate over its alternatives. From the standpoint of all usual standards of decision theory, adoption of G_1 can in principle emerge as the rationally superior option. In such a situation there is nothing inherently irrational about adopting an unattainable goal.

The pursuit of goals is a course of action. And whenever a course of action can (at comparatively low cost) enhance the prospect of achieving a good overall result, it is rationally warrantable. For we face the situation of Display 2.

The expected values of the situation indicate that the indicated action is warranted whenever

$$p(r) + (1 - p)r' > p'(r) + (1 - p')r'$$

or equivalently

$$r(p - p') > r'(p - p')$$

Seeing that $r > r'$ by hypothesis, this relationship will obtain whenever $p > p'$ (so that $p - p'$ is positive). As long as an ac-

Display 2 A SCHEMATIC CHOICE SITUATION

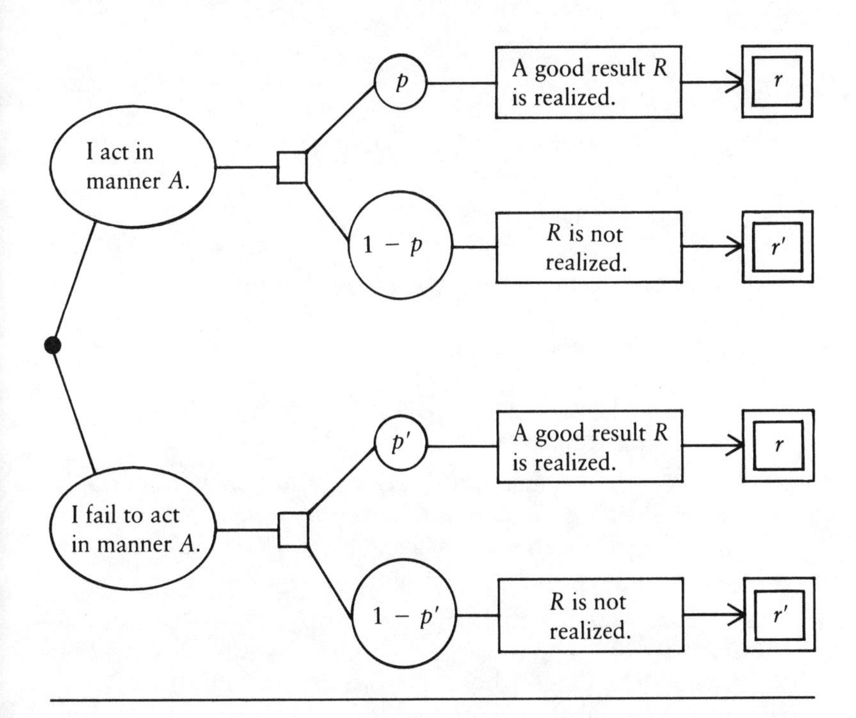

tion or course of action contributes (at a comparatively low cost) to enhancing the probability of attaining a good result, it is rationally well advised.

The key point is simply this: Rationality is a matter of the intelligent exploitation of our opportunities in the cultivation of the good, and nothing prevents the pursuit of impossible goals from forming an integral part of this overall effort. The quixotic pursuit of a recognizedly lost cause can instantiate that seeming foolishness which is allied to genius. As F. Scott Fitzgerald wrote, "The test of a first-rate intelligence is the ability to hold two opposed ideas in the mind at the same time, and still retain the ability to function. One should, for example, be able to see that things are hopeless and yet be determined to make them otherwise."[3]

8. Conclusion

These deliberations indicate that a cogent rationale for adopting and pursuing an unattainable goal can be developed along (at least) the following two lines:

(1) As a component element of a holistically unified, wider goal structure, which also incorporates other appropriate desiderata that indeed are achievable. (This would validate this impossible goal as something whose pursuit yields desirable and desired associated side benefits apart from those directly at issue in the goal itself.)

(2) As a way to maximize actual achievement in circumstances where the adoption of other cognate goals that are less ambitious and more "realistic" would actually be less productive.

Commitment to a recognizedly unattainable goal may be perfectly rational in cases where this has "redeeming features"—when there is a positive rationale for its adoption and pursuit wholly apart from the (unavailable) benefits that would be yielded by its prospective (but actually unattainable) realization.

To be sure, this general way of justifying the pursuit of unachievable goals is essentially instrumentalistic, that is to say, pragmatic and utilitarian. It hinges their validity on their utility—on their capacity to conduce to the realization of certain desired objectives distinct from the (unavailable) goal realization itself. And this relationship has clear implications for the status of unattainable goals in a strictly rational scheme of things—namely, that they can be mediate but not ultimate, fa-

[3] F. Scott Fitzgerald, *The Crack-Up*, ed. Edmund Wilson (New York, 1945), p. 69.

cilitating but not ulterior. Their appropriateness hinges on their systemic utility rather than their individual merits. (But of course this circumstance does not make the pursuit less potentially desirable—or appropriate.)

Admittedly, "Be realistic!" "Don't hitch your wagon to a star, keep your feet on the ground!" and "Don't pursue overly ambitious objectives and set yourself impossible goals!" are perfectly *sensible* pieces of advice. Responsible parents could unhesitatingly urge them on their offspring in perfectly good conscience. And yet the world would be a poorer place if these injunctions were *universally* heeded. Sometimes it is only by setting impossible goals—by striving after the recognizably unattainable in trying to accomplish something one realizes perfectly well to be unachievable—that great things can be achieved. Its unattainability is emphatically not a decisive argument for the irrationality of adopting an ideal.[4]

[4]But does such a validation of unattainable goals as pragmatically well advised not conflict with the principle that "*ought* implies *can*"? Not really! For what is impossible here is not the pursuit but only the achievement. No one is insisting that we are obligated (practically or prudentially) to *achieve* unattainable goals but only that their adoption and cultivation can make good practical sense. ("*Ought* implies *can*" will be examined in the next chapter.)

II

Does *Ought* Imply *Can*?

On Inconsistent Obligations and Moral Dilemmas

Synopsis

(1) Can a duty or obligation obtain even if its discharge is impossible? To investigate this issue, it is helpful to examine the operation of moral rules. (2) To understand the idea of a conflict or "inconsistency" between rules, it is important to recognize that there is a substantial difference between rule inconsistency and the thesis inconsistency that is familiar from logic. (3) Moreover, moral dilemmas can arise even where there is no *conflict* of rules at all. (4) There is good reason to reject the idea that "*ought* implies *can*," and thus (5) to recognize that an obligation can prevail despite the impossibility of its discharge, so that moral dilemmas are an unavoidable aspect of an imperfect world. (6) Kant's thesis that "*ought* implies *can*" represents a principle of ideal-order ethics and does not hold for the suboptimal realities of an imperfect world. (7) A system of moral rules that did not allow dilemmas to arise would thereby be rendered unserviceable in "the real world."

1. *Introduction*

The opening chapter maintained that it is not irrational to aim at the unachievable. The present one extends this line of thought in a somewhat different direction. Its object is to argue that an obligation is not necessarily abrogated by the impossibility of its accomplishment. Not only, then, is the unachievable not automatically to be shunned, it may even turn out to be morally obligatory in some circumstances.

A convenient starting point toward this unorthodox destination is provided by the widely held negative view regarding those moral codes—systems of moral rules—that allow inconsistent obligations to arise. This view is predicated on a position that runs essentially as follows:

> There is something seriously wrong, indeed actually *irrational*, about adopting a system of ethical (or other sorts of practical) rules that admit of conflicts—rules that will, in certain circumstances, issue mutually inconsistent rulings. The very circumstance that such a code can engender inconsistent results in some situations renders it ipso facto inadequate and marks its adoption as irrational.

In contrast to this approach, it will be argued here that the very reverse is the case: that it would be inappropriate to demand a system of ethical rules that did not permit this sort of "inconsistency" to arise. Moral dissonance is not a disaster. An insistence on rules that did *not* allow this to occur would actually be counterproductive and contrary to reason, because the prospect of allowing moral dilemmas and inconsistent obligations—of admitting ethical "contradictions"—serves an important positive function in any viable system of moral rules.

2. *Rule Inconsistency versus Thesis Inconsistency*

Some preliminary observations about inconsistency are in order.

The idea that consistency is a basic requisite of rationality is accepted without question on virtually every side. Philosophers of the most widely discordant persuasions hold in unaccustomed unison that something contrary to good sense and sound reason occurs when we fall into inconsistency in *any* situation.

However, this widely prevalent idea fails to reckon properly with the profound difference in the way that the conception of inconsistency is generally applied to *rules* on the one hand and to *theses* on the other. In assertoric logic, a set of theses (axioms or other statements) is said to be inconsistent if there is *no* set of circumstances in which these propositions are cosatisfiable—in which *all of them can* be realized concurrently. But established usage so operates that a set of rules is said to be inconsistent if there is *some* set of circumstances where they are not cosatisfiable—in which *not all of them can* be realized concurrently. With inconsistent *theses,* these items are not corealizable in *any* situation; with inconsistent *rules,* these items are not corealizable in *some* situation.

A great disparity accordingly obtains between the two cases of thesis inconsistency and rule inconsistency.[1] "Never cosatisfiable" is clearly far more problematic than "not cosatisfiable in some circumstances." Very different things are at issue. And so the ominous connotations of "inconsistency" in the case of assertoric theses do not carry over to the case of prescriptive rules. It is by no means utterly catastrophic for rules to be inconsistent in the sense now at issue. In fact quite the reverse is the case. There is good reason—so we shall argue—why this circumstance should actually be welcomed.[2]

[1] One of the few to remark on it is Ruth Barcan Marcus, "Moral Dilemmas and Consistency," *Journal of Philosophy* 77 (1980): 121–36, esp. 128–29.

[2] In his "Moral Realism and Moral Dilemmas," *Proceedings of the Aristotelian Society* 80 (1979–80): 61–80, Samuel Gutenplan confronts the inconsistent quartet:

(1) If moral realism is to be tenable, the case of the moral descriptor "ought to obtain" must be isomorphic with the case of the alethic descriptor "does obtain."

(2) There are no alethic ("is true") dilemmas.

Display 3 A DILEMMA

You borrow $100 from *X* and $100 from *Y* (in relevantly similar circumstances, so that there is no question of precedence or priority of obligation). The day before repayment is due, you are (contrary to all reasonable expectation and without any fault or failing on your part) deprived of all your assets beyond $100. Without committing any blameworthy acts, you are placed by unkind fate into a situation where you cannot repay all your debts.

Theses:

(1) You owe $100 to *X*—that is, you are validly indebted to him for this sum. (By hypothesis)

(2) You owe $100 to *Y*—that is, you are validly indebted to him for this sum. (By hypothesis)

(3) You ought to repay (all) your debts. (Obligation-establishing rule)

(4) You ought to repay $100 to *X*, and you can. (By (1), (3))

(5) You ought to repay $100 to *Y*, and you can. (By (2), (3))

(6) Your repaying $100 to either creditor is—in the circumstances—*incompatible* with your repaying $100 to the other.

3. *Incompatible Obligations and Ethical Inconsistency*

Consider the concrete instance of a moral dilemma set out in Display 3. Here you clearly have a conflict of duties, being so

(3) There are moral ("ought to be") dilemmas.
(4) Moral realism is tenable.

Gutenplan's way out of this inconsistency is to reject (3) and to join the fraternity of those who, with Kant, deny the prospect of moral dilemmas. (Only fleetingly—namely, on page 64, where he considers the *must* vs. *should* distinction—does he glimpse the easier way out of rejecting, or rather qualifying, premise (1). When "moral realism" is seen in a suitable perspective, there remains no reason why moral realists should feel compelled to deny moral dilemmas.

A different approach is that of Richard Routley and Val Plumwood in "Moral Dilemmas and the Logic of Deontic Notions," *Discussion Papers in Environmental Philosophy* 6 (Canberra, 1984). They effectively deny (2), taking recourse to a paraconsistent logic in the alethic case. The rejection of (4) is yet another option, though one we ourselves find unappealing.

situated that carrying out one of your duties is (in the circumstances) flatly *incompatible* with carrying out another.

This example is interesting because it shows that ethical dilemmas need not result from a *conflict of rules*. A single rule—thesis number (3)—can suffice to generate the problem, without any collision between discrepant rules. Accordingly, a principle of collision-avoidance among rules is not sufficient to avert ethical dilemmas. Setting priorities among moral rules or among classes of "valid moral reasons" for acting will not do the needed job.

To be sure, as one contemplates the preceding situation, one observes that there is nothing actually *self-contradictory* about this sort of ethical dilemma as such. Problems of *outright* inconsistency—of strict *logical* incompatibility—will only arise when we introduce some further theses that are not substantive moral prescriptions enjoining particular obligations but higher-level ethical principles governing obligations in general. Specifically we can add two of them:

(i) You should honor *all* of your obligations. And so, if you are obliged to do *A* and obliged to do *B*, then you are obliged (inter alia) to do both *A* and *B* together. (The Principle of Combination[3])

(ii) *Ought* implies *can*: an obligation only exists where the possibility of its fulfillment is present. Incapacity defeats obligation. (The "*Ought* Implies *Can*" Principle)

[3]Bernard Williams calls this "the agglomeration principle," but I prefer a somewhat more prosaic terminology. See Bernard Williams, "Ethical Consistency," *Proceedings of the Aristotelian Society,* Supplementary Volume 39 (1965): 103–24, reprinted in his *Problems of the Self* (Cambridge, England, 1973), pp. 165–66; and *Moral Luck* (Cambridge, England, 1981), esp. the chapter on "Conflict of Values," pp. 71–82. Williams rejects the principle with a view to such oft-considered counterexamples as Sartre's case of the young man who feels obligated, on the one hand, to join the resistance forces and, on the other, to care for his aged mother. Such cases seem to tell against the principle, seeing that the two actions invoked are clearly incapable of combination. But this move is usually parried by denying that real obligations are at issue.

Note now that, in Display 3, theses (4) and (5) together will, given (i), entail that you ought to repay both *X* and *Y*. This yields by way of (ii) that you *can* do so. And this in turn conflicts with thesis (6). The situation has become really serious, for we have now arrived at an actual logical contradiction.

It is at just this point—when one comes to the question of how to avert such hard-line inconsistency—that ethical theorists manage to paint themselves into some pretty tight corners.

Some hold that we must abandon the Principle of Combination. As Ruth Barcan Marcus puts it:

> Just as "possible *P* and possible *Q*" does not imply "possible both *P* and *Q*," so "*A* can do *X* and *A* can do *Y*" does not imply "*A* can do both *X* and *Y*." [Accordingly] . . . it must also be maintained that "ought" designates a morality that cannot be factored out of a conjunction. From "*A* ought to do *X*" and "*A* ought to do *Y*" it does not follow that "*A* ought to do *X* and *Y*." Such a claim is of course a departure from familiar systems of deontic logic.[4]

The range of theorists who take this way out includes Bernard Williams and Bas van Fraassen.[5] (Barcan Marcus herself merely *considers* this policy of rejecting "the principle of deontic distribution" without actually endorsing it.)

Despite its able exponents, this course is rather problematic. One major shortcoming is that it is totally counterintuitive. The plain man, the commonsense moralist, and a great cloud of philosophical witnesses would never question the Principle of Combination. "What sort of 'obligation' can you possibly be thinking of," they would scornfully ask, "if it does not hold that you are obligated to fulfill collectively your several distributive obligations?" If any second-level principle of moral obligation is ever plausible, this one is it.

[4] Ruth Barcan Marcus, "Moral Dilemmas and Consistency," p. 134.

[5] Bernard Williams, "Ethical Consistency," and Bas van Fraassen, "Values and the Heart's Command," *Journal of Philosophy* 70 (1973): 5–19.

Other theorists accordingly take a different course. They do not abandon the validity of the Principle of Combination as such but merely deny its applicability to the case in hand. They reason as follows:

> Owing someone $100 does not engender an actual obligation (duty) to repay that debt. When you borrow that $100 and promise to repay it, you take on, not an obligation as such, but only a prima facie obligation. You do not commit yourself to repay. You only commit yourself to repay if it is possible for you to do so (and you commit yourself to do nothing that will foreseeably impede your capacity to repay and thus preclude this possibility). And so, it is not actually your duty (obligation) to repay but only your duty (obligation) to do what you reasonably can do toward realizing this end. The obligation you have is not absolute but only conditional.

Those who take this line accordingly deploy this distinction, taken from W. D. Ross, between *actual* (or absolute) and *prima facie* (or conditional) duties and obligations.[6] Actual obligations are definitive and peremptory; prima facie ones are provisional and defeasible, subject to being overridden by strong counter-considerations that render them inoperative. Deploying this distinction, Ross and his congeners insist that in standard obligation-generating transactions like borrowing and promising, the latter rather than the former sort of obligation is invariably at issue. In such a view, a "rider of normality" attaches to all moral injunctions. "You ought to repay your debts" is to be construed as "In all normal circumstances, you ought to repay your debts." We now systematically avoid actual dilemmas because dilemmatic situations are, by hypothesis, extraordinary.

This line of reasoning has significant attractions. First and

[6] W. D. Ross, *The Right and the Good* (Oxford, 1930), especially the chapter "What Makes Right Acts Right?," and *The Foundations of Ethics* (Oxford, 1939), pp. 84–86. Compare Azizah al-Hibri, *Deontic Logic: A Comprehensive Appraisal and a New Proposal* (Washington, D.C., 1978), pp. 41–49.

foremost among these is that it enables us to deny that there is such a thing as a conflict of duties at all. Whenever duties *seem* to conflict, we say that what is at issue is not an actual duty at all, but merely a prima facie duty. Moral dilemmas are illusory—the result of an illusion created by insufficiently exact thought that has not clarified where real duty lies.[7] Real duties just do not conflict. As Kant put it: "A conflict of duties and obligations is inconceivable (*obligationes non colliduntur*)."[8]

But this position also has major liabilities. The most serious of them is that it simply devastates commonsense morality. The plain man just does not use or admit this weasling distinction between *actual* and merely *prima facie* duties. For this distinction leads to the anomalous result that there is no possible way for us to perform an act that produces an obligation. No promise, no assurance, no commitment, no guarantee can be taken at face value. No action we take will engender a duty; literally *nothing* one can do creates an actual obligation. The concept of obligation now simply vanishes from the domain of moral agency, to be replaced everywhere by the idea of provisional and prima facie commitment. The shadow of qualifications such as "if I can," "if it is possible," "if circumstances do not prevent," and the like falls across all our efforts to assume obligations.[9] All our assurances are fair-weather assurances. The failure to bind oneself unqualifiedly—already characteristic of modern marriage—now pervades the whole range of ethical commitment. That well-meaning attempt to avert moral dilemmas

[7] This, in effect, is the position of Terrance C. McConnell's paper "Moral Dilemmas and Consistency in Ethics," *Canadian Journal of Philosophy* 8 (1972): 269–87. When moral dilemmas (seemingly) arise, the flaw lies wholly in our imperfect understanding of the duties of the case: "an adequate moral theory must not allow for genuine dilemmas" (p. 287).

[8] Immanuel Kant, *The Metaphysical Principles of Virtue,* trans. James Ellington (New York, 1964), p. 24 (*Akad.* 6, p. 224).

[9] Some moralists do indeed take such a line. According to Seneca, for example, the proviso "if nothing happens to prevent it" dogs the commitments of the virtuous man at every step. See F. H. Sandbach, *The Stoics* (London, 1975), p. 44.

Display 4 A MORAL PROBLEM

X has incurred (quite unproblematically) a debt of $100 to *Y*. The day before repayment is due, his (*X*'s) assets are embezzled (or stolen or destroyed or otherwise annihilated). By no fault of his own, unforseeably and wholly without culpability of any sort, he is placed in a position where he cannot repay.

Theses:

(1) *X* promised to do *A* (i.e., repay *Y* that $100).

(2) *X* finds himself (due to unexpected circumstances wholly beyond his control) unable to do *A*.

(3) Promises engender obligations: one ought (is morally obliged) to keep one's promises. (Obligation-establishing rule)

(4) "*Ought* implies *can*." And consequently, by conversion, "*cannot* entails *need not*." Incapacity defeats obligation. ("*Ought* Implies *Can*" principle)

---

would gravely undermine the sense of obligation in the moral community.

Yet another recourse remains to enable us to escape from inconsistency. We can reject the principle that "*ought* implies *can*."[10] To motivate this (ultimately appropriate) rejection, it is useful to consider a situation somewhat different from that of the preceding conflict-of-duties case.

4. "Ought *Implies* Can" *Revisited*

Let us contemplate the moral problem set out in Display 4. It is clear here that the four theses at issue constitute a *logically* inconsistent quartet: the conjunction [(1) & (3) & (4)] entails not-(2). Something has to give.

There is precious little we can do about theses (1) and (2). They simply obtain by the characterizing hypothesis that sets

[10] E. J. Lemmon takes this course in "Moral Dilemmas," *The Philosophical Review* 71 (1962): 139–58, esp. p. 150. Ruth Barcan Marcus, "Moral Dilemmas and Consistency," also rejects the principle.

out the factual parameters of the case. We must turn elsewhere.

One possible way out is to abandon thesis (3)—to jettison the Obligation-establishing Rule at issue. The only semiplausible way to do this is to resort once more to the aforementioned distinction between actual and prima facie obligations. One would accordingly weaken thesis (3) to the contention that promises engender only prima facie obligations. But this approach is not satisfactory; we have already commented on its substantial shortcomings.[11]

As we now look to other possibilities, an interesting fact emerges. The Principle of Combination is not involved in *this* dilemma at all. Its abandonment or modification accordingly does us no good on the present occasion. To abandon it is to pay a price that fails to yield the expected benefits. To see it as pivotal is to become diverted by what is simply a red herring.

In this light, then, we come down to thesis (4). Abandoning the principle that "*ought* implies *can*" emerges as the only remaining option. Is this option open to us?

In actual fact, what is at issue is not that we simply *abandon* the principle of "*ought* implies *can*," but that we *modify* it. To see how this can be done, let us take a closer look at the principle.

"*Ought* implies *can*" amounts to "obligation implies capac-

[11] In a recent essay ("Consistency in Rationalist Moral Systems," *Journal of Philosophy* 81 [1984]: 291–308), Alan Donegan proposes to convert apparent situations of moral conflict (or overdetermination) into situations of moral underdetermination. Morality often does not tell you what to do (it does not tell you what career to choose), and it does not tell you what to do in dilemmatic situations either. The fireman has the obligation to save *somebody* in the burning building—either *A* or *B*—but neither specifically. His duty is wholly discharged by saving one of them. Analogously Donegan would (apparently) say of Dilemma No. 1 (Display 3) that your duty is wholly done by repaying *either X or Y*—this being all that you can possibly do in the circumstances. Such an approach would indeed eliminate any conflicts of duty and salvage the principle that *ought* implies can. But the resultant position seems counterintuitive to say the least. It introduces an element of disjunctive randomness into the discharge of duties that simply is not there in the setting of presystematic morality. On Donegan's approach, you do not give duties and obligations to individuals, you simply agree to "put them on the list."

ity," which in its turn is equivalent to "incapacity removes obligation." And this formulation suggests that something rather problematic is afoot. Two considerations serve to make this clear:

(1) To all appearances, an obligation can persist despite an incapacity. We constantly have to be prepared to say things like "He has the obligation/duty to do *A*, although in the circumstances he unfortunately cannot do it." We have to be prepared for the prospect of undischargeable duties and unmeetable obligations—for commitments that cannot be kept through life's accidents.

(2) While incapacity does not actually defeat an obligation, it can, however, negate all blame for a failure to carry it out. Incapacity does not remove an obligation as such; what it does do is to provide us with a potentially valid excuse for not discharging it.

This second point is crucial. What an incapacity can do is to render failure to honor an obligation *venial,* provided there is no culpability in engendering that incapacity and no possibility of foreseeing that the default would come about. Of course, an incapacity does not excuse a default when it is a *culpable* incapacity, a self-imposed inability contrived deliberately by the agent to avoid having to honor an obligation. (Having volunteered for a dangerous mission, he drugged himself as the time approached.) Nor does the incapacity excuse default in cases of predictable incapacitation when it could have been foreseen in advance that the agent would become incapacitated. (For example, a person undertakes to help a friend even though he is aware that his superiors will shortly send him elsewhere.)

The salient point is simply this: you *ought* always to do your duty (to fulfill your obligations). But sometimes you just *cannot* because unforeseen circumstances preclude. And when this happens—when fate turns uncooperative—it is not that the duty is annihilated, but rather that your failure to discharge it becomes excusable. You are exempt from blame if you are "the victim of circumstances"—if your incapacity to do as you ought is due entirely to eventualities that you could neither control nor foresee. When this occurs, the obligation is still there, but your failure to honor it is now nowise culpable. There is no basis for recrimination or reproach. The default at issue does not constitute fault or wrongdoing. All the same, that duty retains its force; its burden remains in place.[12]

There is no arguing with the thesis that it *ought* to be the case that you always do your duty. This is something quite unproblematic ("*ought* implies *ought*"). But it does *not* engender "*ought* implies *can*"! Sometimes you just cannot do your duty; it is simply not possible in the circumstances. But this fact does not undo the duty as such. It just means (or rather, in the proper conditions it just *might* mean) that your failure to do your duty is excusable—that no blame or recrimination can reasonably be attached to your failing to act as you are indeed obligated to. Failure to do one's duty, though always regrettable, is not automatically blameworthy. Such failures can be culpable or venial as the case may be.

As we assimilate cases of conflicts of duty with cases of inability to perform duties, we come to acknowledge that moral dilemmas can be perfectly real: that (despite Kant) obligations can indeed collide. But it also means that in such cases a failure to honor obligations may well entail no personal fault. We arrive once again at a recognition of the tragic condition of man—that there will be circumstances in which we must excuse his defaults because he simply *cannot* do as he ought.

5. Moral Dilemmas

Exactly this line of thought can also be adopted in resolving the moral dilemmas we have been contemplating—and the myriad

[12] People are not only enmeshed in moral dilemmas through transgressions of their own. An unkind fate can propel them there as well. One cannot say of you in the context of Dilemma No. 1 (Display 3) that you should not have incurred those debts at all because matters might conceivably so eventuate

conflict-of-duty cases that lie in their environs. In such cases one can and should say that the agent indeed *ought* to honor those incompatible obligations, but, unfortunately and regrettably, cannot do so in the existing circumstances (which were nowise of his making). To be sure, this fact does not *annihilate* the duty or obligation. It exists and remains. But the agent's failure to do as duty demands, to honor his obligation, is venial. His default must be excused: it is real, but pardon-deserving.

This sort of approach makes it reasonable to take a hard line on moral dilemmas. We can accept them as part of real-life reality,[13] acknowledging that we do really encounter moral dilemmas in the real world. Situations arise where acting in good faith and conscience can nevertheless mean that, when "things go wrong," we cannot fully honor all our obligations—that "ought" is not *removed* but merely *frustrated* by "cannot." We can acknowledge the reality of moral dissonance and accept that this is simply a fact of life that reflects the tragic nature of the human condition.

In the real world we have limited resources of time, money, energy, and opportunity. If we run unexpectedly short, or if misfortune strikes us, our opportunity for adequate action is limited. I promise to do something for you, but illness prevents. I undertake to attend the meeting, but the bus is unexpectedly delayed. I incur various financial obligations, but unforeseeable misfortunes prevent their discharge. Those obligations all stand—undischarged and violated. But they do so without morally adverse effect: I remain free of any blame and merited reproach.

In life we can without impropriety—and indeed must—gear our commitments to reasonable expectations and stand ready to enter into obligations that might possibly become unmeetable

---

that you cannot honor them. For if this line held good, the morally upright person could never undertake any obligations whatsoever. The whole project of morality would become infeasible.

[13] This, in fact, is the line taken by some, such as Bernard Williams, "Ethical Consistency," and Ruth Marcus, "Moral Dilemmas and Consistency."

"if worst comes to worst." Virtually any two moral rules can come to be parties to a conflict of duties if matters work out badly enough. But the unkindness of fate does not destroy our obligations as such; it does no more than render venial our failures to honor them. Its effect is not to transmute a dereliction of duty into a nonviolation thereof, but simply to make that violation excusable. And so, when dilemmas arise, this does not mean that the rules were not authentic rules of obligation, but only that there can be circumstances in which we can default on obligations without incurring blame or moral opprobrium.

Obligation, commitment, and responsibility can outrun the reach of the possible. The commander is "responsible" for *everything* within his command; his obligation and his goal are to ensure that *all* goes well. But of course he cannot actually control everything. Again, the captain is responsible for the safety of his ship, and this obligation does not cease to exist when its effective discharge proves impracticable because unforeseen circumstances impede. For example, the captain's responsibility for the safety of his passengers may outweigh or override his responsibility for the security of his vessel—his duty to the passengers may overwhelm his duty to the ship and its owners. But that does not mean that those overridden obligations are set at naught. They continue in force, albeit subordinated and overshadowed in the conflict, but extant all the while. As such, a moral dilemma is nothing paradoxical; it is merely an especially difficult case of moral conflict, of the general phenomenon of divergent ethical pushes and pulls.

The morally unfortunate fact of life is that people often cannot avoid having to leave their obligations undischarged. When such a default of duty occurs without any actual fault, there often still remains a "moral remainder"—a residue of unsatisfied obligations that make room for warranted regret, appropriate remorse and self-reproach, and residual duties to compensate and atone insofar as possible. Moral dilemmas are *misfortunes:* they admit of no morally perfect solution, only resolutions that are (at best) morally acceptable as lesser evils.

And here a moral residue always remains, still unsatisfied and undischarged.[14]

And so, obligation survives incapacity: *ought* continues in place after *cannot* has come upon the scene. Only by keeping those duties alive, by not letting them become unravelled in the face of incapacities, can we account naturally for all those residual obligations that remain when duties cannot be discharged. Such obligations include those moral demands to atone and to make good as best we can the defaults into which unkind fate has impelled us. When, oversleeping, we wake up two minutes before the time at which we should keep an appointment four miles away, we can say without problem or paradox, "I should be there two minutes hence—I really *ought* to be there—but I just can't."[15] At this point a whole host of "damage control" obligations leap into being (e.g., to phone an explanation and apology).[16]

Moral dilemmas arise when it turns out that several distinct obligations are not cosatisfiable in the circumstances. Moral misfortune arises when matters so eventuate that an obligation is not satisfiable in the circumstances. The present approach is simply to assimilate the former category to the latter—to treat moral dilemmas as potentially just another case of moral misfortune. We thus avert the need to introduce any sort of special machinery to accommodate dilemmas. (After all, *any* adequate

[14] We are often told things like "It would be . . . pointless to suggest that . . . [someone] ought to do something which, for quite general reasons, was, and was certain to remain, not within his power" (G. P. Henderson, "'Ought' Implies 'Can,'" *Philosophy* 61 [1966]: 101–12, esp. p. 101). But there may well be a perfectly good point—namely, to emphasize those residual duties that survive an undischargeable obligation and leave "loose ends" behind.

[15] This example is given by G. P. Henderson, "'Ought' Implies 'Can,'" p. 105.

[16] Bernard Williams has emphasized this Achilles' heel of the standard duties-cannot-conflict theories. They will, he notes, "not do justice to the facts of regret and related considerations; basically because they eliminate from the scene the ought that is not acted on" ("Ethical Consistency," in *Problems of the Self* [Cambridge, England, 1977], p. 175).

ethical theory must, as such, already have the means for accommodating moral misfortunes.)

If our oversleeping is due to no fault of ours (we were not just too lazy to set the alarm; we were drugged by a wicked opponent), our default is wholly excused. But that initial obligation is not cancelled. It remains as the hook from which those residual obligations are derivatively suspended.

To be sure, we must now recognize two different modes of moral injunction: the weaker mode of "should" (*debet, soll*) and the strong mode of "must" (*oportet, muss*). After due allowance has been made for conflicts, obstacles, impediments, etc.—after providing for all those (potentially conflicting) oughts and shoulds—there remains the question of the bottom line. Just what (if anything) is it that, *all* things considered, the agent *must* do in the existing circumstances if the overall interests of morality (or, from another standpoint, prudence or political interest or whatever) are to be served? And at this final end of the line—in the concrete situation in which literally *everything* significantly relevant has been taken into account—what the agent *must* do has to be something that he *can* do. By the very nature of what is at issue with this ultimate "must" of concrete guidance—of "operating injunctions"—ought-dilemmas cannot be replicated at the level of must-dilemmas. But of course this "bottom line," which has to make allowance for all the conditions and circumstances of particular cases, cannot be what is at issue in a moral rule. Such rules of duty or obligation appertain not to a situation-specific *must* but to a generic *ought*.[17]

We thus arrive at the distinction between mere "*duties*" on the one hand and "all-things-considered moral *requirements*" or "moral *mandates*" (as one author calls them[18]) on the other. To get from duties to imperatives of action—to determine ca-

[17] On *must* versus *ought*, compare E. J. Lemmon, "Moral Dilemmas."

[18] Earl Conee, "Against Moral Dilemmas," *Philosophical Review* 91 (1982): 87–97, esp. p. 92.

suistically just what it is that we ultimately "must" do in the circumstances—is often a long story. It can never be told simply in terms of the rules themselves but requires a look at their situation-specific bearing within the conditions and circumstances of particular cases.[19]

The crux is the question of our stance toward the moral rules themselves. Compare the metarules:

(M1) You *should* follow the moral rules—you *should* honor all of your obligations.

(M2) You *must* follow the moral rules—you *must* honor all of your obligations.

Here (M1) is unproblematic and incontestably appropriate. But (M2) encounters difficulties. For cases will occur where (to all appearances) you just cannot follow (all) the moral rules because that just is not possible in the circumstances. And so we face a choice. We can weaken (M2) to:

[19] But are there not simply the translational equivalences:

Present Terminology	*Ross Terminology*
duty	prima facie duty
bottom-line duty	duty

Do these distinctions not run strictly parallel so that the difference between the two positions is one of terminology alone? Not really. For the basic issue is that of the nature of ethical rules. The fact is (1) that it is the job of rules to specify what our duties are, and (2) that rules as such *in principle cannot specify bottom-line duties*. And this just does not square with Ross's terminology; he is constrained to say that rules inevitably operate at the prima facie level.

This stance that the rules specify only prima facie duties, not duties as such, just does not do justice to the spirit in which moral rules are issued and received. Prima facie duties just do not carry the force of obligations—they are too soft and defeasible. The shift to prima facie obligations makes it difficult to account for the residual obligations that remain when we are prevented from doing what duty demands—the obligation to do what one can to make up for one's defaults.

(M*2) You *must* follow the moral rules insofar as possible—you must do as much as you possibly can toward discharging all of your duties.

Or we can retain (M2) as is but weaken what the moral rules themselves demand by reconceptualizing them as stating prima facie requirements. The thrust of this discussion is to insist on the former strategy. Its stance is: "Keep the moral rules intact as principles of categorical obligation. But recognize that amid the harsh realities of an uncooperative world, we sometimes have to 'compromise' our demands on rule obedience." The logic of the situation constrains a choice between:

(1) Absolutistic rules with the "realistic" expectations of a weaker metarule (M*2),

and

(2) "Realistic" rules (as weakened by the shift to a prima facie level) with the absolutistic expectations of a stronger metarule (M2).

And the first alternative is preferable here because it involves a minimal revision of our natural ways of talking in this domain.

The fundamental principle is that what you *must* do has to be something that you *can* do. Accordingly, (M2) would call for saying that only the feasible things one actually can do can count as (genuine) obligations. By moving to (M*2), we avert this consequence. We need no longer say that a duty ceases to be such when its discharge becomes infeasible. But, of course, we now face the consequence that duty alone can no longer tell us what we *must* do—that rule morality is not in itself a sufficient determinant of morally appropriate action.

The moral rules spell out our duties. In doing this they purport to provide us with good (moral) reasons for action. But there is a difference between an isolated reason and a comprehensive balance-of-reasons that provides for a result in which "everything has been taken into due account."

The gulf between a morality of general principles as defined by rules and the bottom-line rulings of appropriate moral judgment is substantial. Rule-delivered prescriptions and proscriptions do not go far enough by themselves. For *any* action can be salvaged by redeeming features—by being, under the circumstances, the lesser of two evils. Any act, however heinous in the eyes of rule morality, can in principle be rendered appropriate "in the final analysis" if it in fact represents the optimal alternative in the prevailing circumstances. It is only at the level of casuistical bottom-line morality—and emphatically not at that of a generalized rule-morality—that something like "*ought* implies *can*" obtains.

The salient point is that *ought* does not entail *must;* having a certain duty does not automatically constitute a preponderant moral reason for action. Those mandatory "bottom-line" obligations of course cannot conflict (ex hypothesi); at *that* level there are no moral dilemmas.[20] But of course to address the issue at this level is unhelpful, seeing that "bottom-line" duties and "conclusive moral reasons" are no more than terms of philosophical art. The root problem arises at the pretheoretical level of the plain man's duties and obligations as defined by the moral rules. And here, moral dilemmas certainly can and do arise.[21]

6. *The Kantian Aspect*

In his *Metaphysic of Morals,* Kant writes as follows:

> A conflict of duties (*collisio officiorum sive obligationum*) would arise if one could (wholly or partially) cancel the other.

[20] See Earl Conee, "Against Moral Dilemmas."

[21] The present analysis is close at many points to that of Roger Trigg's paper, "Moral Conflict," *Mind* 80 (1971): 41–55. Trigg's approach to moral dilemmas seems closer to the position of common sense than that of most recent writers on the subject.

> But since duty and obligation in general are concepts that express the practical necessity of certain actions, and since two opposing rules cannot be necessary at the same time, then, if it is a duty to act according to one of them, it is not only not a duty but contrary to duty to act according to the other. It therefore follows that a conflict of duties and obligations is inconceivable (*obligationes non colliduntur*).[22]

Kant deems a conflict among duties impossible, since in his view the course of duty is paramount and simply annihilates its rivals. A "duty" will, as such, "express the practical necessity of certain actions." The preponderate duty is the only one there actually is, and it hardly makes sense to speak of a conflict where a single party stands alone on the battlefield.

The present approach sees the matter in a rather different light. The fact that some duties overshadow or suppress others does not mean that these others are annihilated and set at naught. They remain living and active—they *ought* to be obeyed and honored, even though in the circumstances they *need* not be because conflicting duties momentarily overshadow them. Moral dilemmas are real and painful precisely because those conflicting duties all remain alive and active—and unsatisfied.

This perspective indicates that it is *not* the case that "*ought* implies *can*" so that *cannot* abrogates *ought*. In the real world, an "ought" may well survive and persist even after, owing to some unhappy twist of fate, "cannot" enters upon the scene.

But this line of thought calls not for simply *abandoning* Kant's principle but rather for its proper reinterpretation. If matters went smoothly—if things always worked out well and everything turned out according to an ideal plan—then obligation-impeding surprises would never occur. In an *ideal* order of things *ought* would indeed imply *can*. If all went well, and un-

[22] Immanuel Kant, *The Metaphysical Principles of Virtue*, p. 24 (*Akad.* 6, p. 224).

kind fate did not make hash of our best-laid plans, then Kant's principle would in fact hold good. The helpful bystander would now never have to choose which of two drowning infants to rescue. People would never be born into Sartrean situations, where duty to family and to country come into conflict. The only sort of moral dilemmas that could arise if fate were never unkind would be those of an agent who undertakes explicitly conflicting obligations—who, as it were, perversely engages himself to serve two incompatible masters. And *such* cases, of course, can arise only through morally inappropriate actions.

The upshot, then, is that *ought* ought to imply *can*. In an ideal order of things there would be no moral dilemmas. If "nature" were cooperative (in not forcing potentially conflicting obligations into actual inconsistency), and if agents acted rightly (and did not enter into explicitly inconsistent obligations), then moral dilemmas would vanish from the face of the earth.

The pull of contrary duties is simply a hard fact of life in an imperfect world. When all goes well, obligations to friends and to employer, to family and to country, to oneself and to one's fellows are smoothly cosatisfiable.[23] But when things go ill, when the demands made somewhere along the line become excessive, then we are simply forced by malign fate into having to default somewhere along the line.

In *this* sense Kant was quite right. In the *ideal* (rather than real) world—in the sort of world a benevolently right-minded agent would wish for, nay, would actualize if he could—adequate ethical rules cannot generate dilemmas. Being unproblematic in *such* a world would indeed be a condition of adequacy for such rules. Rules that can lead into difficulties in a benign world—where there are no surprises on nature's part and where

[23] A variety of philosopher's textbook examples of such situations are enumerated in the 1984 monograph by R. Routley and V. Plumwood, "Moral Dilemmas and the Logic of Deontic Notions."

all its occurrences go predictably "according to plan"—would thereby manifest their own untenability.

In the ideal (Kantianly *noumenal*) realm, then, *ought* indeed does imply *can*. And if, with Kant, our interest is in ideal-order ethics—in the moral order as such rather than in its casuistical implementation in the imperfect realm of uncooperative phenomena—then we are perfectly entitled to the supposition that "*ought* implies *can*." But it is only in the context of his primary concern for ideal-order morality that Kant can say flatly that: "A conflict of duties and obligations is inconceivable."[24] What Kant offers us in the second *Critique* (and in the *Grundlagen* as well) is a perfectly good theory of moral obligation, but it is one that obtains only for ideal-order morality. It is an ethic geared to the situation of an ideal world, not to the unpleasant realities of the actual one. (It is, of course, rendered relevant to our real-world situation through the prime moral imperative to work toward actualizing an ideal order.)

To be sure, Kant himself is well aware that our moral duties are always imperfect in the suboptimal setting of real-world ethics. He himself recognizes and stresses that ethical theory cannot designate practical rules for determining the specific right action that properly discharges all of the agent's moral duties in a particular case:

> Ethics, because of the "slack" that it allows for its imperfect duties, inevitably leads the faculty of judgment to decide how a maxim should be applied in particular cases; and since the answer gives us another (subordinate) maxim, we can always inquire again after a principle for applying this maxim to other cases that may arise. And so, ethics falls into "casuistry."[25]

And in *The Ethical Doctrine of Elements,* where Kant treats the

[24] Immanuel Kant, *The Metaphysical Principles of Virtue,* p. 24 (*Akad.* 6, p. 224).

[25] *Ibid.,* p. 71 (*Akad.* 6, p. 412). I have slightly revised the translation.

various particular duties of virtue, he considers casuistical questions, which he often leaves unresolved. But the fact remains that in those discussions where the doctrine of "*ought* implies *can*" is preeminent, Kant's deliberations proceed (appropriately) at the ideal level.

As Kant sees it, only in the ideal order does the rule ethic of obligating grounds (*rationes obligandi*) afford a framework for actual obligations (*obligationes*). He makes a good deal of this distinction. The passage with which this section began continues as follows:

> A conflict of duties and obligations is inconceivable (*obligtiones non colliduntur*). But two [opposing] grounds of obligations (*rationes obligandi*), one or the other of which is inadequate to establish an obligation (*rationes obligandi* [*sed*] *non obligantes*), may well be conjoined . . . for in such a case one of the grounds is not a [real] duty. When two such grounds are in conflict, practical philosophy does not say that the stronger obligation prevails (*fortior obligatio vincit*) but that the stronger ground of obligation prevails (*fortior obligandi ratio vincit*).[26]

None of this creates the slightest difficulty from our perspective. Kantian "duties" cannot conflict because in the ideal world they are "the bottom line" in that they "express the objective practical necessity of certain actions." But in the real world the rules that set out our *rationes obligandi* can conflict in difficult and problematic circumstances. And at this point moral *reasoning* alone is unable to settle the matter. We need the difficult art of compromise that moral *judgment* affords. (Here, as elsewhere, Kant's distinction of "faculties" does yeoman work for him.)

7. *Acknowledging Dilemmas*

In abandoning "*ought* implies *can*" in its unqualified construction, we acknowledge the insufficiency of ethical rules to deter-

[26] Immanuel Kant, *The Metaphysical Principles of Virtue*, p. 24 (*Akad.* 6, p. 224).

mine conduct in the real world. For actual conduct is inescapably conditioned by *can*; it is a truism that we can only succeed in doing what actually can be done. And in those cases where *ought* runs afoul of *can,* the ethical rules as such may well not be in a position to determine action. They are rules of *ideal* preference and this may not suffice to determine action in *sub-ideal* cases where moral dilemmas arise and the rules of ethics may well fail to decide matters.

Consider once more those problem cases mentioned at the outset. What is to be done in such conflict-of-duty situations? We temporize, we compromise, we resort to damage containment—we strive to minimize harm and to make the best of a bad show. We can indeed obtain help from further ethical principles like "Treat like cases alike." But when all this is said and done, many alternatives still remain. (Pay each party $50; flip a coin to decide who gets his $100; impel them into negotiation.) It is not that the ethical rules provide no guidance at all, but that they are underdeterminative and do not constrain one particular resolution. We have penetrated into a region where all that the ethical rules can do is to provide guidelines but not answers.

The fact that there can be moral dilemmas and conflicts of duty in the recalcitrant world we actually inhabit does *not* mean that there is anything inadequate about the rules of morality as such. For those rules do not—and cannot reasonably be expected to—tell us what to do in circumstances where we cannot do everything that we ought to do in their light. A code of ethics provides guidelines rather than procedural instructions. It is not an *algorithm* for determining what to do in the difficult conditions of real life. It *delimits* the range of acceptable actions (provides for constraints), but it does not necessarily determine particular acts.

We are now at last in a position to return profitably to the chapter's starting point and consider the (mistaken) idea that there is something wrong with a system of ethical rules that permits moral dilemmas to arise. We shall do this by way of an argument from general principles in support of the idea that an adequate body of moral rules actually has to be dilemma-admitting. To be sure, we will not maintain that allowing dilemmas is essential to the *theoretical possibility* of a set of moral rules. Rather, we will argue that this is required for the *practical efficacy* of such rules—that it is essential to the capacity of such rules to do the sort of job for which moral rules are instituted.

The most that moral rules can effectively succeed in doing is to specify the factors we should take into account in our moral deliberations. By their very nature they cannot determine a moral *mandate* adjusted to the vagaries of endlessly variable circumstances. Rules govern *should* but not *must.* And as long as this is so—as long as they are not endlessly context-specific—the rules can never avoid the prospect that the circumstances are such that the action they prescribe fails, in the particular context at issue, to avert some preponderant evil. The guidance of rules is never enough "for all practical purposes."

Consider what a family of moral rules would have to be like that did not allow moral dilemmas to arise. A dilemma-excluding set of moral rules would have to be such that, given some (i.e., *any*) combination or permutation of moral obligations or duties that an agent might have (naturally or by voluntarily entering into them) *and any concatenation of events that would preclude their full concomitant realization,* then these rules would have to decide some one particular unique resolution. The rules would have to determine a uniquely obligatory course of action that would in fact satisfy all the "demands of duty" amid the welter of conflicting duties and complicating circumstances of concrete situations. The duty-defining rules would thus have to be sufficiently complex that a determination of one's duties would become endlessly fine-tuned to the concatenation of prevailing conditions so as to be in a position for a resolution to the question "But what am I obliged to do in *these* particular conditions—what does duty demand here and now?" To preclude any prospect of conceivable clash, the rules would have to provide for the endless variation of conceivable circumstances. The rule-framer would have to do the job not of the legislators alone, but of the trial judges as well.

But if the rules were *that* complicated, it would become effectively impossible for anyone to *formulate* them—let alone to *learn* them. Our body of moral rules would be of incomparably greater length and complexity than the operating instructions for a battleship or the manual of regulations for operating an airline. Any code of civil or common law devised over the ages would be like a drop in the ocean compared to the manual of morality. And this volume of complexity would be altogether fatal to the capacity of the rules to do the sort of job for which a moral code is instituted among men. For it is a prime function of a moral code to guide people into smooth and mutually beneficial patterns of interrelationship with each other. To do the sort of work that is at issue here, the moral rules have to be learnable "at mother's knee." A system of morality (like a system of language) must be something that a person of average intelligence can pretty well master in its essentials by the age of seven or eight.

A moral code is perfectly entitled to recognize the quotidian realities of this world and thereby to place some reliance on the fact that by and large things go well enough for people to be in a position to honor their commitments and discharge their obligations. Such a code can—and must—rely on the fact that reality is by and large benign—that surprises are the exception, not the rule, in human affairs.

If it were overly complex, a moral code could not survive as a living force in the community of men. It could not preserve itself in place through transmission from generation to generation. Its maintenance would have to be the work of a special elite—a trained priesthood of experts. Its ability to function and to regulate our doings and dealings with one another in the interactions of everyday life would become totally unstuck.

An ethic of rules must be a manageably sized family of injunctions of the form: "In situations that meet condition *C*, do *A*." And the difficulty is that even though doing *A* is appropriate in most cases when condition *C* obtains (or in all *standard* cases when this is so), it is never *always* appropriate. Adverse conditions can always result in a nonstandardness that makes following the rule inappropriate *in this case*. And no set of learnable rules can possibly take all permutations and combinations of possible adversity into account.

The task of discerning, amid the particular circumstances of a difficult world, the best way out of our moral perplexities belongs not to rule morality but to its judgmental (i.e., casuistical) application. The application of the rules and principles amid the vagaries of concrete situations always requires reference to detail—and to more detail than can ever be encompassed at the level of general rules. The striking point lies not in the general rules themselves but in their concrete implementation. When following the rules itself leads us into difficulties, the problem becomes one of resolving issues with the least overall harm—damage containment. And for the conduct of *this* enterprise, rules themselves do not suffice. Here we cannot proceed by moral reason alone; we also require judgment.

Rules are necessarily generic in orientation: they can only specify types of obligation. And any given type of obligation can always be overridden in special cases, such as when its default turns out to be the lesser of the evils. Rules can only specify the generalities of action. But particular acts must be performed in concrete circumstances whose ramifications can never be encompassed *in toto* by any set of rules. A system of moral rules that did *not* "oversimplify" matters would through this very fact become unworkable.

Accordingly, all that a family of moral rules can do is to provide general guidelines. Rule morality in this view can indeed orient and guide but cannot determine and specify action. The rules cannot give us detailed instructions for what to do under endlessly complex and varying conditions and circumstances. A moral code has to be substantially less complex than the Code of Justinian or the Napoleonic Code. All it can do—and all it need do—is to give us guidance in ordinary or standard circumstances. The rest it can (and must) leave to our sensibility and our good sense of the spirit of the enterprise. Even as a code of laws must always leave room for the work of judges, so must a moral code leave room for the work of the casuist.[27] By itself it provides not *instructions* but *principles;* it sets out the strategy without detailing the tactics.

And so it is mistaken to deem it irrational to adopt a body of rules that allows the possibility of conflict. Rule inconsistency is something very different from thesis inconsistency and is, in contrast, essentially harmless. The prospect of conflict in out-of-the-ordinary cases is the price that any set of rules—moral codes included—pays for the sort of simplicity that is essential to its capacity to function effectively in the guidance of conduct. Only an "inconsistent" body of rules can be anything like satisfactory in adequately accommodating the complexities of the real world.

If a system of rules did *not* admit the prospect of moral dilemmas and conflicts of duties—if it had the sort of internal richness and complexity that could even begin to preclude the prospect of moral dilemmas—then it could not be the sort of thing a moral code is, and would not be able to perform effectively the job that it is instituted to accomplish. Interestingly, it is in the interests of its *practicability* that an ethic of rules must remain, in substantial degree, an ideal-order ethic that abstracts from the potentially infinite complexities of real life.

As these deliberations indicate, the fact that a certain task cannot be carried out in the circumstances at hand will not of itself unravel its status as an obligation. *Cannot* does not necessarily imply *need not.* A call to duty can outrun the limits of

[27] To be sure, this work should properly be the job of the agent himself: it is neither necessary nor desirable to hand it over to a special class of experts.

the possible. Even a rule ethic can make room for the conception of an obligation that is not destroyed by mere infeasibility—and can thus permit of "impracticable ideals." An ethic of rules is not inherently antithetical to one of ideals, precisely because it itself provides for an ideal that is in fact unrealizable amid the harsh realities of a difficult world—that of a person who altogether "lives by the rules." The moral enterprise is fundamentally committed to the never fully achievable task of making a place for the ideal in the hostile environment of the world's realities.[28]

[28] Some of the ideas of this chapter were refined in discussions with Geoffrey Sayre-McCord.

III

MAXIMIZATION, OPTIMIZATION, AND RATIONALITY

On Reasons Why Rationality Is Not Necessarily a Matter of Maximization

Synopsis

(1) There is a widespread tendency to construe rationality in terms of utility maximization—to think of rational choice as a matter of maximizing something called "utility." (2) But quantitative measurability is a prerequisite of meaningful maximization, and the exchangeability or convertibility among items of worth is a precondition of their measurability. This condition is certainly not met in general, since there is no common unit of equivalency for diverse aspects of value. (3) "Utility" is at best a useful fiction. The penchant of economists to the contrary notwithstanding, real human goods are not commensurable in terms of a common sort of "utility," in the way in which different commodities can be priced in terms of a common "money." Accordingly, the rational choice among various alternatives of value (or disvalue) cannot be conceived of as a process of meaningful maximization. (4) Rational choice is a matter not of one-dimensional *maximization,* but of the structurally diversified *optimization* that calls for harmonizing a complex profile of diversified goods and goals. (5) A utility theory that abandons the

link of utility to value—that takes utility as a mere index of preference rather than a measure of preferability—thereby also severs the link between maximization and rationality. When utility no longer reflects what is in someone's real interest, there is no longer any good reason to regard maximizing it as "the rational thing to do." (6) Some combinations of goods are simply unrealizable in the real world; some value profiles are literally "too good to be true." To bring them into view we have to resort to idealization. And this raises a question: Can a recourse to such ideals be squared with the demands of reason?

---

1. Rationality and Maximization

There is a widespread tendency to construe rationality in terms of maximization, taking rational choice to consist in maximizing something called "utility." Practitioners of economics, social choice theory, game theory, management science, and other exponents of "the theory of rational decision" generally unite in inclining to this approach of construing rationality in terms of utility maximization.[1] They commonly hold that the rational man always aims at some kind of measurable good (a "utility" correlative with "satisfaction" or "well-being" or some such) and that he chooses among alternatives for action in such a way as to maximize the expectation of its realization, endeavoring to "maximize expected utility" as the economists' cliché has it.[2]

[1]See, for example, D. M. Winch, *Analytical Welfare Economics* (Harmondsworth, 1971): "We assume that individuals balance rationality and endeavor to maximize utility" (p. 25); and compare Kenneth J. Arrow, *Social Choices and Individual Values*, 2d ed. (New York, 1963), pp. 3, 21. Some, to be sure, take exception to this line. For example, it has received a sophisticated critique in Herbert Simon's well-known proposal of a shift from maximizing to "satisficing."

[2]As one discussion puts it: "The theory of games is a valuable tool in making more determinate our understanding of rational self-interest. For the solutions it provides . . . [enable people] to maximize their expected utilities, or in other words, their expected well-being." R. D. Luce and H. Raiffa, *Games and Decisions* (New York, 1957), p. 200.

Philosophers of widely different ethical orientations agree in taking this same general line. Utilitarians identify rationality with utility maximization outright.[3] And contractarians too see rational men impelled to a consensus regarding the ground rules of social interaction in an endeavor to maximize their satisfaction.[4]

Is this view of rationality as utility maximization defensible? Given that rationality is a matter of reasoning appropriately about what is to be done by way of belief and action, can one proceed to see this as a matter of maximizing a certain sort of thing?

One issue must be put aside straightaway. There is, of course, a perfectly trivial sense in which rational men are maximizers. For presumably they endeavor *ex officio* to maximize the extent to which they behave rationally. This truism is not in question—and not to the point. Of course, rationality is a matter of doing what is most appropriate and most intelligent. But the question at issue is: *What sort of thing is that?* Does this intelligence and appropriateness itself call for maximizing something of a particular sort? Can all our ends be amalgamated, fused together into a single all-embracing measurable good, one all-inclusive mode of merit?

To be sure, members of an achievement-oriented society who strive for a maximum of performance and success are card-carrying maximizers. But then so are those lazybones who always try to get by with the very least that will meet the requirements of the situation. They are simply maximizing something else—say, energy conservation. No matter what you do, you can

[3] See John Stuart Mill, *Utilitarianism,* chap. 3.

[4] Cf. Kurt Baier, *The Moral Point of View* (Ithaca, 1958), pp. 308–15. Often it is *morality,* not just mere *rationality,* that contractarians see as emergent from good-maximization: "The two main concepts of ethics are those of the right and the good. . . . Now it seems that the simplest way of relating them is taken by teleological theories: the good is defined independently from the right, and then the right is defined as that which maximizes the good" (John Rawls, *A Theory of Justice* [Cambridge, Mass., 1971], p. 24).

be a maximizer—namely, someone who maximally approaches to the behavior pattern of a person who acts like *that*. There is not all that much glamour in the abstract idea of maximization as such; the interest lies in the issue of just what is to be maximized.

And it is here that we come to that elusive commodity of "utility" which, so we are told, provides the fuel that runs the engine of rationality. But this view that rational agents are utility maximizers has deep problems. If taken seriously to apply to rational agents in the real world, rather than as characterizing that useful fiction, the "economic man," then this conception of rationality in terms of utility maximization runs into difficulties. An examination of these defects can throw light both on the nature of rationality itself and on the objects of our particular present concern—ideals.

2. *Incommensurable Goods*

The conception of rationality as utility maximization is predicated on the plausible idea that the quintessentially rational thing to do is to promote the good of man—to enhance human well-being. But, sensible though this may seem, it does not validate a recourse to "utility." For human goods and satisfactions are something complex and variegated. They not only come in different *sizes* (as measurable in terms of volume or of realization likelihood), but they also come in different *kinds* as well. The sphere of human values is a complex and pluralistically diversified realm.[5] And this raises difficulties.

The idea of *maximizing* the good rests on the presupposition

[5] As one recent writer sensibly puts it: "Value has fundamentally different kinds of sources, and they are reflected in the classification of values into types. Not all values represent the pursuit of some single good in a variety of settings." Thomas Nagel, "The Fragmentation of Values," in his *Mortal Questions* (Cambridge, England, 1979), pp. 131–32.

that all of the different items of value at issue can be evaluated by a common, uniform measure. It makes no sense to think of literally *maximizing* the good when we cannot measure goods by a common standard. *Commensurability* is basic to the project of value maximization. And hereby hangs a problem.

Goods are commensurable only if—despite their evident *seeming* to be of different kinds—they can all be assessed in terms of a "common denominator." Different shares of them thereby differ as to value only in point of different quantities of this common denominator—in exactly the way in which baskets of apples and of oranges differ in (monetary) value only in terms of their price. Commensurability presupposes a common unit in which all value-relative comparisons can be conducted in the way in which all money-value comparisons can be effected in terms of a market price. Convertibility in terms of this neutral and pervasive "common denominator" (e.g., price) is crucial to commensurability.

Convertibility, however, is nothing universal—it reflects a situation of very restricted generality. Different kinds of goods are not necessarily convertible. Consider some of the points of merit of a car: maximum speed, starting reliability, operating reliability (freedom from breakdown), passenger safety, and economy of operation. If the top speed of a car is 1.75 MPH, no augmentation in passenger safety or operating reliability makes up for this shortcoming. Again, if the car is eminently unsafe, an increase in its other virtues cannot offset this. Where the various merits of a car are concerned, there simply is no free exchange among the relevant parameters, but only complicated (nonlinear) trade-offs over a very limited range.

This example illustrates a general situation. There are very different ingredients to goodness, qualitatively different value aspects, different sorts of good-making factors. This much we may take as a given. But what are we to assume about the prospect of combining these value parameters into an overall result—a single, everything-taken-into-account, synoptic "bottom line"? In principle one might suppose that there is a synthetic "function of combination" of the following sort:

(1) It provides an ordering that assigns to every value-parameter combination a place in a "synoptic preferability ordering" of some sort.
(2) This ordering is not a mere *partial* ordering but a full-fledged *linear* ordering, so that every two situations are comparable in point of overall preferability.
(3) This linear ordering is not a mere comparison ordering but an actual *cardinal* ranking, so that preferability can be weighted in point of more or less and fitted out with a full-scale quantitative evaluation as a matter of (measurable) degree.

But just how far can one legitimately move down this list? The position we take here is positive and favorable with respect to point (1), skeptical with respect to point (2), and negative and unfavorable with respect to point (3). And this last point is the crux. It is not against (potentially partial) comparability that our argumentation is directed but against measurability as such.

But perhaps point (2) is after all the real pivot because one can move *automatically* from preferability to mensuration, thus making much capital from the fact that we just about always have *preferences* in situations of choice. Confronted with alternatives and constrained to choose among them, we will almost invariably come up with *something*. Can one not then effect a shift from mere ordinal preferences to actual cardinal utilities by suitably ingenious contrivances to operate with preferences? Some economists think one can. They invoke the machinery of probabilities to effect this transition and propose to construct a person's utility rate-of-exchange between diverse items *A* and *B* from his answer to questions of the form:

> Would you prefer an *x* percent probability of obtaining *A* to a *y* percent probability of obtaining *B*?

Following the lead of John von Neumann, these theorists hope to exploit such probabilistic preferences to extract outright utilities.[6] But this approach to utility extraction rests on an "indifference condition" of probabilistic commensurability that for any two desired items *A* and *B*, there are probabilities *a* and *b* so proportioned that there is indifference between an *a* percent chance of *A* and a *b* percent chance of *B*. And just this supposition is unrealistic.

In the final analysis the convenient recourse to probabilities does not help matters all that much. For to trade chances of different goods makes sense only if we would be prepared to trade these goods themselves at some rate of exchange—only if they themselves are commensurable through interchangeability. And exactly this supposition is questionable and problematic.

The commensurability of goods presupposes their exchangeability or convertibility. But goods are not always convertible. The good of man is fundamentally multiform, composed of radically diverse components—comfort, affection, security, understanding, etc. People want and need different kinds of goods, and no overflow of one can make up for a shortfall of the other. If here and now it is information I really need and want, I will not trade a library for "all the tea in China." The idea of convertibility is thus unrealistic. It presupposes that, in relation to any two goods *A* and *B* whatever, we will unhesitatingly trade one unit of *A* for *n* units of *B*, for some suitable value of *n*. The condition of things must be such that it just does not matter to us which of two kinds of particular goods we get, because the addition of more of the one can always make up for the diminution of the other.

For the economist there is nothing all that problematic in this. He is accustomed to the assumption of a *market* that establishes exchangeability and underwrites a price mechanism to provide a general standard of comparison. For him, it is normal and

[6]See John von Neumann and Oskar Morgenstern, *Theory of Games and Economic Behavior,* 2d ed. (Princeton, 1947).

natural to suppose that different goods can be evaluated in terms of a common unit—money. He can equate the value of x apples with that of y oranges, because the price mechanism yields a rate of exchange to establish convertibility between them. For him, accordingly, exchangeability in a market can be invoked to provide for commensurability. But this envisions a very special set of conditions.

There are many examples of significantly valuable human "goods" in which there is no market. Consider, for example, life, liberty, and happiness. Once slavery is outlawed, life and liberty are no longer marketable. Only up to a certain (inherently limited) point is health purchasable. It is proverbial that "money can't buy happiness." And there are many other important things it cannot buy, such as true friendship or the affection and respect of those about us. Walpole to the contrary notwithstanding, it is doubtful that "Every man has his price." Again, it is important to us that our children be capable and hardworking, that our neighbors be neighborly, and that our colleagues be cooperative. But none of these desiderata are marketable. It is easy to forget how special a case is at issue with the exchangeability of goods. No sensible person would be prepared to put all of his eggs into the basket of one single sort of goods. (As wiser theoreticians have always realized, the dispositions of "economic man" do not pervade the whole spectrum of human life.)

Economists, decision theorists, and their congeners are powerfully attracted to the thesis:

> Value is homogeneous: there is at bottom but one single kind of value—"utility." All other modes of value are ultimately reducible to this.

If this were so, if value were homogeneous, then rationality would indeed be a matter of maximization—of simply maximizing "utility." But that is just not the way it is. We must reject the dogma of the *homogeneity of value.*

To be sure, life would be much simpler if all goods were in fact commensurable. I would not have to fret about my choices in difficult cases—would not feel "in a dilemma" about them—if everything could be measured in a common unit that provides for automatic comparability. But that just is not the way it is in the real world.

In general, things have many different value aspects V_i, and we have no function of combination V to extract a single, all-embracing *measure* of overall value from them. We have to deal with a plurality of distinct "parameters of value." Even if we assume (perhaps rashly) that measurability is possible *within* each of these parameter dimensions, there need be no way of making quantitative comparisons across different value parameters by way of weighing them off against each other in a common scale.

Economists themselves have long seen that it is deeply problematic to try to combine the several ordinal preferences of a group's individual members into an overall collective ranking of the utility of this group of valuers.[7] But they have been much slower to recognize the (closely analogous) point that it is just as problematic to combine the utility values (or preferability indices) *of the several diverse facets of a single object* into a synoptic measure of its overall utility (or preferability). All of those notorious difficulties about the comparability of the cardinal utility (or the comparative preferences) of diverse individuals recur quite analogously in the case of the comparability of the measurable value (or the comparative preferability) of an object's diverse value facets.[8]

Even if we grant that one alternative of a spectrum is generally

[7] See Kenneth J. Arrow, *Social Choice and Individual Values* (New York, 1951; Cowles Commission Monograph no. 12). And compare Otto Neurath, "Das Problem des Lustmaximums," *Jahrbücher der philosophischen Gesellschaft der Universität Wien* 18 (1912): 182–96.

[8] Compare the attempt to develop a "multiple-attribute utility theory" in Ralph L. Keeney and Howard Raiffa, *Decisions with Multiple Objectives: Preferences and Value Tradeoffs* (New York, 1976).

preferable to its rivals, this still does not mean that its being so is a matter of possessing more or less of some mysterious something called "utility." To think of utility in that sort of way is to engage in an illicit reification or hypostatization. The economists' idea of pervasive "utility" is about an order of magnitude more problematic than the IQ testers' idea of a pervasive "intelligence." There just is no monolithic sort of something of such a sort that something preferable is ipso facto equipped with more of *that*—"more X-affording" with respect to some one single, homogeneous, ubiquitous desideratum. The idea of a generalized utility in whose terms preferability is always embedded is a mere fiction—sometimes useful (for example, where a "market" exists), but by no means universally applicable.

The economists' utilitarian idea of the homogeneity of the good is ultimately untenable. The idea of a single all-governing standard of value, even one so seemingly protean as "utility" or "satisfaction," is too simplified and undiscriminating in its vision of the good as something internally so uniform in composition as to admit of the commensurability of its constituent components. There simply is no one single common measure for diverse aspects of value.

3. *Utility Maximizing Is Not Generally Feasible*

Let us now conjoin the preceding points in interactive juxtaposition:

(1) The commensurability of goods—their lending themselves to a literal *measurement* in terms of a common unit of worth—is a precondition for any meaningful maximization.

(2) The commensurability of goods presupposes their mutual convertibility (be it in volumetric or in probabilistic terms).

(3) The "goods" at issue with many significant human values are of substantially different qualitative kinds. They lack

> the common denominator needed for interchangeability and, consequently, just are not mutually convertible.

When these three points are conjoined, the thesis that the rational pursuit of "the good of man" is a matter of maximization comes to grief. The rational choice among items of value (or disvalue) cannot be conceived of in terms of maximizing some single universal mode of value reflected in an omnipresent "utility."

One recent writer says: "The identification of rationality with maximizing activity requires . . . [that] we suppose that there is a single measure of a man's ends, which can be applied to evaluate the contribution of each of the actions possible to him."[9] Just so! But this means that people should put a measurable value on any possible object of choice in terms of a single common yardstick of appraisal—that the good be seen as ultimately homogeneous. And this demand is unreasonable and unrealistic.

Many forms of evaluation—of assessing the comparative merit of goods—cannot be reduced to measurement. We cannot *measure* the quality of a dramatic performance or of a meal. We can, of course, measure what people are prepared to pay for such things, but that carries us back to the special conditions of a market.

Maximizing is inevitably a matter of "getting as much as one can" of something. The maximization idea has no bearing otherwise. Only where the goods at issue can be compared through appraisal in terms of one single homogeneous value does it make sense to pursue ends by way of maximization. When we lack a

[9] David Gauthier, "Reason and Maximization," *Canadian Journal of Philosophy* 4 (1975): 411–33, esp. p. 415. As I see it, Gauthier's painstaking defense of the thesis that rationality consists in utility maximization is essentially circular, since it is predicated on a definitional construction of "rationality" that is manipulated to lead to this result. For analogous criticisms of this line of approach, see Max Black, "Making Intelligent Choices: How Useful is Decision Theory?," *Dialectic* 39 (1985): 19–34.

common standard and confront a plurality of distinct and non-exchangeable values, none of which simply predominates over the rest, the idea of maximization is of little avail.

In general, the convenient option of maximization is accordingly denied us. Where there is no quantitative measure, the idea of maximizing based on the comparison of more or less has no application. It makes little sense to ask "Who is the better athlete, a world-class discus thrower or a world-class high-jumper?" or "Who is the better musician, a good cellist or a good trombonist?" We can, of course, compare them in point of quickness, dexterity, steadiness, and other such particular physical skills and talents. But these are mere *prerequisites* for excellence at athletics or musical performance, not *components* thereof. When measuring them, we do not measure the end product in whose realization they cooperate.

The characteristics of the *general* case are as follows.

(1) There are various substantially distinct parameters of value—various distinct *kinds* of goods.

(2) They are not mutually convertible.

(3) We require them in contextually varying amounts and combinations. Every value parameter must be present to *some* extent in any acceptable situation. A minimum threshold obtains with respect to these value dimensions. (With a car, for example, some minimal threshold of speed, reliability, safety, etc. must presumably be assured before we would be prepared even to consider the item as acceptable.)

(4) Within the range of "acceptable" cases (in the sense of point (3)), comparative preferability is a complex matter of coordinating pro and con considerations in a way that is *not* a matter of maximization of some sort. Everything depends on contexts and combinations.

In sum, "the good" at large is multidimensional, not homogeneous. Enhancing it is a matter of optimizing a profile, not of maximizing a quantity.

To be sure, we can have (perfectly sensible) preferences in such matters. But there is no particular something of such a sort that "preferable" or "better" comes down to having more of this something so that preferability is somehow geared in this way to maximization. We can have *standards* in such cases, but not *measures*. We can have criteria of preferability, but not criteria that proceed by quantitative measurements of some sort (any more than do our standards of "good literature"). And where there is no measure, there can be no maximization either. The rational choice among alternatives of value (or disvalue) cannot be conceived of in terms of maximizing some single all-pervasive and universal mode of goodness.

The kingdom of interests is large and diversified. No one type of good and no single preponderant value rules the realm of appropriate ends. Their character is diversified, their bearing variegated, their character heterogeneous, their weight incommensurable. We must recognize the reality of a diversified spectrum of legitimate ends. No one, all-predominant summum bonum is in operation. No single uniform good-making factor is uniformly present throughout all goods in a way that leads them to differ merely in degree rather than in kind.

Utility maximization is accordingly a special-purpose instrument of significant but substantially limited application. To construe rational choice in terms of maximization is entirely inappropriate in its supposition that the special case of general exchangeability among parameters of value is somehow typical (or even universal). The theoreticians' "utility" is a problematic hypostatization that is useful in some limited contexts—say when exchangeability is feasible—but has no unrestricted validity.

People constantly make rational decisions in driving their cars, investing their assets, choosing their careers, tidying up their closets, purchasing their food, etc. Throughout, they are doing all sorts of well-advised and intelligent things—saving money, prolonging longevity, enhancing comfort, enlarging their friendships, enhancing their knowledge, etc. But to say that they are throughout doing exactly the same sort of thing—promoting "utility"—is an eminently problematic contention. The idea of a single all-enhancing good is an oversimplification—a heritage of the monolithic summum bonum thinking of bygone days.

Realistically viewed, rational choice is a matter not of unidimensional maximization but of multidimensional optimization. It remains a matter of determining what is preferable. But here the preferability at issue need *not* necessarily reflect itself in some quantitative way through the operation of some *measure* of value such that

(M) A pref A' if and only if $V(A) > V(A')$

Once we realize that there are different modes or aspects ("dimensions") of value, and that they bear differentially on different ranges of comparison, we can no longer be confident that preferential valuation can be reduced to mensuration.

If condition (M) held, preferability would invariably be transitive. But it just is not. Consider a (micro)range of objects of comparison *A, B,* and *C*. If we compare *A* and *B*, within this (micro)range, the apposite standard is *a*. Then we shall (so let us suppose) arrive at the assessment that *A* is preferable to *B*:

a: *A* pref *B*

However, when we compare *B* and *C*, the standard that is appropriate to this particular comparison range may be *b*, and we will then have (so let us suppose):

b: *B* pref *C*

But if we now turn to *A* and *C*, the appropriate standard will be C, and we may well have:

c: *C* pref *A*

But there is now no possible way to provide for *these* assessments in terms of an overall measure. For any value measure over the range A, B, and C would have to yield a *transitive* order of preference, whereas the given preferences are clearly *not* transitive. And this sort of thing is not just a theoretical possibility but something that can perfectly well happen. Consider a concrete example:

(1) I am asked: "Do you prefer butter or olive oil?" I respond: "Butter." For I reason that in contexts where this sort of choice makes sense—namely, in cooking or frying—I prefer butter.

(2) Next I am asked: "Do you prefer butter or mayonnaise?" I respond "Mayonnaise." For I reason that in contexts where this sort of choice makes sense— namely, in sandwich-making—I prefer mayonnaise.

(3) Now I am asked: "Do you prefer mayonnaise or olive oil? I respond: "Olive oil." For I reason that in contexts where this sort of choice makes sense—namely in dressing salads—I prefer olive oil.

It is clear that this sort of nontransitivity can always be expected in cases when different "perspectives of consideration" cast their independent ballot,[10] so that preferability is context dependent and point-of-view dependent. And this is pretty well *always* the case. Thus suppose that someone had objected at step (1): "You really should not have said that you prefer butter to olive oil if you don't so prefer it in *all* cases." This invites the

[10] The considerations at issue here run parallel to those involved in M. S. A. de Condorcet's "Voting Paradox" in the theory of rational decision. Condorcet's paradox occurs when we obtain cycles in a group preference determined on the basis of majority-rule voting with respect to pairwise comparisons. An example of this occurs when three voters indicate the following preferences among any items a, b, c: (1) $a > b > c$, (2) $b > c > a$, (3) $c > a > b$. Note that two (i.e., a majority) prefer a to b, two prefer b to c, and two prefer c to a. See the Marquis de Condorcet's *Essai sur l'application de l'analyse à la probabilité des décisions rendus à la pluralité des voix* (Paris, 1785; reprint, New York, 1973). Compare Isaac Todhunter, *A History of the Mathematical Theory of Probability* (London, 1865; reprint, New York, 1949), pp. 374–75, as well as Duncan Black, *The Theory of Committees and Elections* (Cambridge, England, 1958).

reply: "But that's just foolish. It gears preference to a condition of things that effectively *never* obtains." For our preferences among objects of choice are never unqualifiedly universal and situation independent. I may strongly prefer butter to margarine. But if *A* says to me, "I'll give you a fortune if you give me a bit of margarine here and now," and *B* stands by offering me the free choice between a pat of butter and a pat of margarine, I'm obviously not going to choose the butter! Whenever preference is something situation dependent (and it always is!), we cannot expect our preferences to be transitive.

Think of the game "scissor, stone, paper." If you were to choose stone, I would prefer paper to scissor; if you choose scissor, I would prefer stone to paper; but if you choose paper, I would prefer scissor to stone. That is just how preferability works. It varies with circumstances: which item is preferable turns on the prevailing context. But actual measurement is not like that. It has to be substantially context independent. (It just does not matter whether we measure the length of the building on a hot day or cold, wet day or dry, a workday or a holiday.) The things, processes, and arrangements of this world do not have a utility or preferability in some absolute way; they acquire a preferability in contextual situations that is powerfully context dependent. And by assessing these relational and interactional aspects of things, we are certainly not carrying out *measurements*.

In general, preferability determination just does not hinge on measuring anything. The measurable is context invariant (at any rate to within limits), but the preferable is not. And so it is infeasible, in general, to reduce questions of preferability to matters of measurement.

To be sure, where maximization of the good is possible, it is clearly sensible and rational to strive for it, other things being equal. That is not in question. The point is simply that the prospect of maximization is *not* always there, and this absence nowise impedes the prospects of rationality.

4. *From Maximization to Optimization: Rational Choice Requires the Harmonization of a Plurality of Goods*

To be sure, what is being denied in these deliberations is not so much the rationality of utility *maximization* as the very viability of *utility* itself as a universal index of worth or value that can be applied to make assessments "across the board."

Rationality is a matter of the intelligent pursuit of appropriate ends. Now this is certainly a matter of selecting "the best option" among alternatives: it calls for so comporting oneself in matters of belief and action as to prefer what is preferable—what *deserves* to be preferred. But when this preferability cannot be quantified—when its determination is a matter of *qualitative judgment* rather than *quantitative measurement*—then rationality ceases to be a matter of maximization.

Diversity is the name of the game where human interests are concerned. The goods and qualities required to sustain a satisfying human life are numerous and varied: food, shelter, liberty and justice, companionship and self-development. Our needs and wants are numerous, diversified—and definitely not interchangeable. No one desideratum reigns supreme. To reemphasize: no single uniform good-making factor is uniformly present throughout all goods in a way that leads them to differ merely in degree rather than in kind.

Rationality calls for promoting a person's real interests, his own welfare specifically included. But improving the quality of a person's life or the condition of a person's well-being is like improving the taste of a particular sort of cake. This cannot be done by simply adding more of this or that ingredient. Central to the whole issue is the problem of blending a plurality of diversified goods into an overall configuration. Rational choice hinges on rational evaluation, and this requires arriving at a suitable *profile* of diverse elements.

Writers who approach the subject from the angle of decision

theory often say things like: "Rationality in the pursuit of goals consists in maximizing the chances of success." But that is nonsense. If *X* is a goal of mine (making a million, say, or landing a certain job), I shall no doubt maximize my chances of its attainment by dropping everything else and concentrating on it alone—to the exclusion of friendship, health, etc. But it is madness, not rationality, that lies down this road. Sensible people do not want to achieve their objective come what may. (Think of the classic short story "The Monkey's Paw" by W. W. Jacobs.) They want success in goal attainment but in a reasonable balance or combination. At most they are willing to prespecify some particular level of commitment and to maximize their choices within the limits set by this level.

Rational agency requires optimization overall—not solving this problem in the *locally* best possible way (of buying the best car I can afford), but in the globally best possible way that takes other commitments and opportunities into account. (Even though the purchase of that car per se is within my resources, its opportunity cost in terms of forgone alternatives may yet be too high.) Rationality is holistic; it is collective optimization rather than distributive maximization that matters.

At this point, then, one comes up against the shortcomings of the concept of economic man and the economists' traditional conception of rationality in terms of the efficient pursuit of prudential self-interest. What the moral philosopher finds particularly objectionable in the proceedings of his colleagues in economics and decision theory is the way they appropriate to their own use the honorific rubric *rationality*. They enumerate certain self-serving principles of assessment—roughly those of atomistically self-interested prudence—and canonize these as axioms of rational decision-making. Such theses are put before us as principles of rationality by fiat or definition or some comparably high-handed act of preemption. We are told with little ado or argument that conformity to a narrowly self-interested modus operandi in choice situations is what necessarily characterizes the choices of the rational man. And, in place of justificatory argumentation, one finds these principles presented as effectively self-evident axioms whose status is virtually definitional—as though such contentions belong to the very meaning of rationality!

When economists, decision theorists, and social choice theoreticians speak so casually of what the rational man does, they manage to conceal under the sheep's clothing of a seemingly descriptive rubric the wolf of a deeply normative commitment, one that is highly dubious and debatable. They arrogate the proud title of rationality from the convenient predilections of their own inherently debatable standpoint.

There is nothing in any way inherently unreasonable or irrational about a selfless concern for others. Indeed, there is no adequate reason for calling a man unreasonable if his actions militate against his own advantage, for there is no earthly reason why he cannot have perfectly legitimate values that transcend his own condition. To be sure, a man will be unreasonable, indeed irrational, if his actions *systemically* impede his own objectives. But there is no adequate ground for holding that his *only* rationally legitimate objectives are of the selfish or self-interested sort. It is a travesty upon this concept to construe *rationality* in terms of prudential self-advantage. To take this stance is to have too narrow a sense of appropriate value. Toward people or nations who have—even to abundance—the constituents of welfare, we may well feel envy, but our *admiration* and *respect* could never be won on this ground alone. Neither for individuals nor for societies is "the pursuit of happiness" the sole and legitimate guide to action; its dictates must be counterbalanced by recognizing the importance of doing those things upon which in after years we can look back with justifiable pride.

Man does not live for knowledge alone—nor pleasure, power, or any other single factor. The catalog of appropriate human values has many entries. Happiness and pleasure are of course on the list (so far the utilitarians are right), but so also are justice, knowledge, wisdom, affection, aesthetic satisfaction, and many others. None of these rules the roost by itself. We want justice but not at all costs (not *fiat justitia ruat caelum*). And there are certainly also limits to the extent to which one could (reasonably) opt for happiness, say, at the cost of self-respect. We confront a variety of desiderata of limited and circumscribed interchangeability.

The intelligent pursuit of one's ends is not simply a question of efficiency. For the matter is also one of balance, subject to the consideration that we must not impede or destroy the prospects of achieving our other coordinate objectives.

The diversity of human goods and values has consequences of great importance. One of these is that there are very *different structures of rationality* because different emphases, different *priorities*, among diverse goods and values are possible and legitimate. We confront a pluralistic situation. For instance, the rationality of the cognitive life is not the same as the rationality of the artistic life. Formal or "pure" rationality may be the same for everyone, but the diversity of legitimate goals for individuals ensures that material or substantive rationality is not.

The rationality of ends is an important and pressing issue precisely because of the diversity of ends. If there were only a single genus of value, the question of the rationality of ends—of adjudging the proper role of each in contexts where the others too are operative—would not arise. It is because there are various alternatives that the question of their harmonization becomes pressing.

Yet if rationality is *not* a project of maximization, then what is it? It is a matter of *optimization* in the pursuit of ends, of doing the sensible thing, of resolving our choices in the most intelligent way possible in the prevailing circumstances. Rationality consists in the intelligent pursuit of appropriate ends—it looks to the *best,* not to the *most.* And this calls for the effective harmonization of a diversified profile of goods in the endeavor to produce an optimal result. But this is not in general a matter of maximizing some quantity. (Doing something "in the most intelligent way possible" may *sound* like maximization, but there is in fact no measurable *quantity* that is being maximized.) Given the inner complexity of the domain of human values, we are constrained to portray the mechanism of rational choice in terms of judgmental *optimization* (of doing "the best"), rather than mensurational *maximization* (of doing "the most"). Optimization is a matter not of "bigger is better" as with maximization, but of balancing, coordinating, and harmonizing goods in one or another of conceivably alternative ways.

Economists and decision theorists often talk as though *all* of a person's wants and preferences were equally rational—as though any end whatsoever were automatically valid (appropriate, legitimate) simply by virtue of its mere adoption. But this rides roughshod over the crucial differences between real and apparent interests.

Consider the sequence:

(i) what I want (here and now)
(ii) what I will want when the time comes
(iii) what I would want if
- I knew more (had ampler information)
- I deliberated more carefully (on the basis of the existing information base)
- I managed to make certain (putatively desirable) changes in myself (i.e., made myself over more fully in the direction of my own ideals)
- I managed to make myself over into a really good person

The further we work our way down this list, the more fully do we effect the transition from actual (or apparent) toward real (or legitimate) interests. The various distinctions operative here (short run vs. long run, well-informed vs. ill-informed, naive vs. reflective, actual vs. ideal) are all crucial for the determination of real as opposed to merely apparent interests. And it is real interests rather than mere wants as such that are central to rationality—not *desiderata* but *desideranda,* not desired things but warrantedly desirable ones. The matter is not what people *do* desire or prefer but what they *should* desire and prefer. The distinction between wants we do have and wants we reflectively feel that it is appropriate for us to have is crucial.

Optimization is a matter of means-ends reasoning: of finding the best overall means to the most appropriate relevant ends. It is a matter at once of efficiency and of teleology. And we must recognize that to optimize—to produce the best overall result—is not necessarily a matter of maximizing anything. As with baking a palatable cake, optimization is not a matter of identifying some particular ingredient or complex of ingredients and then injecting a maximum of that. There just is no identifiable factor or complex of factors such that "better" can be identified with "more of *that.*" The good life, for example, does not consist in a single factor, but involves a blended plurality of goods, such as health, happiness, freedom, companionship, and love. Some are irreducible to the rest in that additions of one are incapable of fully offsetting deficiencies of the others.

Practical rationality is thus no more a matter of maximization than is cognitive rationality. In matters of agency we can "measure the value" of alternatives no more than in matters of belief we can "measure the weight of evidence." In each case, preferability is a matter of *standards* rather than *yardsticks*—of *analysis* rather than *measurement.* We are well advised to resist replacing *deliberation* by *calculation* in an ill-fated indulgence of the "yearning for convenience."

Rationality, then, pivots on "doing the best we can" in a way that is only loosely connected with what is ordinarily understood by "maximization." It is a grave mistake to think that there is some monolithic sort of "goodness" out there for us to maximize. The realm of value is simply too complex for that.

Is the good one or many, homogeneous or heterogeneous? The insight of Plato's *Philebus* holds true here. The good must be construed as a mixture—a matter of blend and proportion, of combining and harmonizing. We return to the root idea of

Pythagoreanism that the good is a *harmony* of a certain sort—a suitable balance of diversified factors. The difference between good music and cacophony does not reside in the fact that the former provides more of something that the latter lacks. "The good" at large is multidimensional, not homogeneous; enhancing it is a matter of optimizing a complex profile, not of maximizing a determinable quantity. Its rational cultivation is a holistic matter of organic harmony rather than a mechanical matter of monolithic maximization.

In a rational choice among (mutually exclusive) alternatives, we begin by determining for each the particular mixture of costs and benefits involved. Comparing these mixtures with one another, we use "judgment" to (try to) find one that is preferable, overall, to all the rest—a process that may well involve procedures over and above calculation. (There may be "weighing" at issue, but it is of a purely figurative sort.) To choose the *overall preferable* result—or at any rate to choose one to which no other is preferable overall—is what reason enjoins, and *all* that reason enjoins. But we may well (and generally do) have to do with a preferability determination in which measurement and maximization as such need play no role whatsoever.

Aristotle was emphatic in insisting that there is no deliberating about valued ends that are ultimate (nonmediate). To deliberate about the appropriateness of an end is to subordinate it to some other end, and this is by hypothesis infeasible in the case of an ultimate end—an ultimate goal or value.

But this doctrine of Aristotle's is simply not correct. For it overlooks the fact that ends can be related to each other in appropriateness-relevant ways that are different from *subordination.* We can deliberate about an end not only on the basis of whether its adoption and pursuit facilitate the realization of some other superordinated end, but also on the basis of its *coordination,* by asking how well it fits into the overall economy of other, associated ends. We can ask about the extent to which their conjoint adoption allows for mutual adjustment and supportiveness. And so we can deliberate about ends not only in the light of other higher ends toward which they are means, but also in the light of value-criteria applied to our "economy of ends" at large—criteria of coordination like coherence and consonance, relative weight or importance (say in the competition for limited resources in the course of their implementation), and the like.

Such issues regarding the formulation of a "rational economy of ends"—issues of compatibility, coherence, consonance, centrality, balance (in point of "weight"), etc.—are not in themselves yet further, different, and "higher" ends. They operate in a different sphere altogether, being values that we import ab extra in appraising our ends at large. They are not ends but value criteria that we deploy to achieve a rational coordination of ends, adjusting them to one another in the light of the fact that rational optimization requires the harmonization of a diversified variety of goods.

The elements of a good journey are not interchangeable: adding more spectacular scenery cannot make up for bad food. Adding more salt (no matter how much) will not compensate for a cake's lack of sugar. The evaluative aspects of the goal are not interchangeable. We must harmonize rather than maximize. In general, when we have to appraise a profile or gestalt of desirabilities, preferability becomes a matter of a contextually determined *structural harmonization* rather than of mensurational maximization. (As the Greeks already realized, the theory of *structure* is just as important as the theory of *quantity*.)

But just how is one to determine the best overall combination of goods in cases of a plurality where no trade-offs are possible? No hard-and-fast rule can be laid down. Different contexts call for different optimizing procedures. To give just one highly schematic example, suppose that for realizing an optimal effect three (individually measurable) goods are needed in the specific proportion 1:1:2. Then if we had to determine whether the combination of 5, 5, 8 units respectively or 7, 7, 7 units is preferable, we would sensibly pick the former over the latter—its aggregate "inferiority" notwithstanding.

Maximization, optimization, satisficing, and similar methods are alternative procedures of "practical reasoning"—of effecting a rational choice among alternatives. Maximization has no monopoly on rationality. Different situations call for different procedures; different processes for the rational resolution of choices are appropriate in different contexts. No doubt, rationality is a matter of opting for the best available alternative. But there is simply no way of transmuting this "best" into "the most of something." (To be sure, we may adopt the trivializing formula of "the most preferable." But what is at issue here is a *façon de parler* that we must not allow to delude us into thinking that preferability is some sort of measurable something.)

5. *Can Utility Theory Abandon the Idea of Measuring Value?*

Science has succeeded in mathematicizing the realm of our knowledge to such an extent that we tend to lose sight of the fact that the realm of our *experience* is not all that congenial to measurement. It is full of colors, odors, tastes, likes and dislikes, apprehensions and expectations, and loves and hates that allow precious little room for measurement. We readily forget how very special a situation measurability is—even in contexts of seeming precision.

But, surely economists will tell us, if you have a preference of *A* over *B*, we can assess its strength by asking: "How much will you pay to ensure having *A* instead of *B*?" And they may well be right in holding that this question can always be asked and often answered. But it does *not* follow that by providing an answer here, one is *measuring* anything—that some independently preexisting quantitative parameter is being measured when we spend hypothetical money to indulge our hypothetical "preferences." A hypothetical market is no more a market than a stuffed owl is an owl. Not everything quantitative is a measure. "How many of those girls remind you of your mother?" you ask me. "Two," I respond. A lovely quantity, that! But what in heaven's name am I *measuring*? Quantification is not necessarily measurement.

But whenever you choose, you indicate a preference, and is the "strength" of such a preference not something measurable? By no means! One frown is severer than another, but I cannot quantify by how much. One girl is prettier than another, but I can put no number to it.

To be sure, someone might object as follows:

> You grant that quantification can be possible without mensuration—that we can assign meaningful numbers in circumstances where we are not *measuring* anything. Is this not really all that utilitarians and their economist congeners want and need?

The answer in the context of our present deliberations with respect to rationality is simply no. That "How much would you pay?" question is pointless in a world of impulse buyers. Its answers, however splendidly precise, are fruitless for the issue of measurement, because they do not represent any sort of independent value parameter—that is, precisely because they do not *measure* anything. And if one cannot see utility as a measure of value of some sort (of something like goodness, acceptability, or desirability), then the linkage between rationality and maximization is broken.

Exactly here is where the approach of most current decision-theoretic utilitarians runs into trouble. They maintain, in effect, something like the following:

> The idea that utility literally *measures* something is hopelessly old-fashioned. Utility is not a measurement at all. It is simply an index of preference. It simply assigns weights to the relative preferences of a person. It does not measure intrinsic preferability, but merely expresses the strength of a like or dislike.

This abandonment of a specific "measurement utilitarianism" enables utilitarians to bypass many of the difficulties surveyed in the preceding discussion. But it purchases this advantage at a substantial cost.

Taking this line, these "mere preference utilitarians" (as we may call them) abandon all claims upon rationality. One person prefers Shakespeare, another the Birdman comics; one gets his pleasure from gardening, another from incinerating moths. Preference as such is simply inclination with no pretense to appraisal and evaluation in the framework of a rational life plan. Any pretense of a linkage between utility and rationality is thus broken.

Clearly, if the use that we propose be made of preference evaluations is to have a bearing on judgments of rationality, then preference must reflect preferability, and there is no basis and indeed no justification for seeing wants and preferences as something final—something outside the pale of appropriate examination and evaluation.

For Bentham and the early utilitarians, utility was *a measure of value*. And so for them the injunction "maximize utility!" was a perfectly sensible answer to the question "What would it be rational for me to do?" But if we join the latter-day economists and decision theorists in disjoining utility from value, in setting up a "value-free" utility theory based on mere preference alone, then utility maximization as such becomes disconnected from rationality. For the question of whether it is *rational* for someone to strive to implement his preferences crucially depends on what those preferences are—whether, for example, he prefers self-inflicted pain or the suffering of others. (The man who prefers that people should think of him as a flowerpot is scarcely rational, no matter how cogently he may labor in this direction.)

The utility-maximization approach to rationality is thus caught in a dilemma:

(1) When utility is approached in the way of the old-fashioned value utilitarians, then rationality could indeed be construed as calling for utility maximization—if only this utility were a well-defined quantity (which it is not).

(2) When utility is approached in the way of the latter-day preference utilitarians, then utility is indeed a feasibly maximizable quantity, but the bearing of utility maximization on rationality is now abrogated.

Either way, the view of rationality as utility maximization comes to grief.

Unless utility can be construed as a measure of *value*, there is no earthly reason to question the rationality of someone who does not bother all that much about utility. But if the quantity at issue is something adventitious—something as inherently insignificant and potentially unreasonable as mere preference or desire as such—then it is simply irrelevant to matters of rationality. Once the link between utility and value is broken, the link between utility maximization and rational choice is also severed. When utility no longer reflects what is in someone's real interest, there is no longer any good reason to maintain that maximizing it is "the rational thing to do."

6. *Ideals and Unrealism*

It lies in the nature of rationality to place a constraint on a person's choices through the distinction that some are rational and others not. To be sure, it is not that certain particular options or actions are, as such, closed off to the rational man—anything can be the lesser of two evils. What is rationally mandatory are not certain actions but certain objectives. The rationality of ends poses an important and pressing issue precisely because of the diversity of ends. If there were only a single genus of value, the question of the rationality of ends—of adjudging the proper role of each in a context where the others too are operative—would not arise. It is because there are various alternatives that the question of their harmonization becomes pressing.

Consider an example. Houses have many different points of merit, such as spaciousness, access to shops and transportation, economy of maintenance and operation, quietness, and privacy of situation, etc. But the world's arrangements are such that these various desiderata come into conflict in actual practice. As spaciousness increases, we lose economy of maintenance and of operation; increasing convenience of access to shops and transportation means decreasing privacy and quiet—and so on. Again, if I want food of great longevity in storage, I must add preservatives that diminish its flavor. Different values can come into outright conflict.

Various combinations of merits are simply not realizable amid the imperfections of "the real world." They involve a degree of perfection that it cannot possibly afford us. As the world's arrangements go, different points of advantage must be balanced off against each other. In practice, different values must accordingly be balanced and harmonized. In practice we must make compromises. But, of course, this fact should not be allowed to undermine our allegiance to values as such.

Just here is where *ideals* come to the fore. An ideal is a thought creature, a product of the circumstance that we can contemplate value conditions beyond the limits of what the actual world can possibly bring to realization. Idealization enables us to press beyond the confines of a reality within which one can only realize some value-enhancing features at the expense of others. Ideals accordingly provide us with a contrast between the inevitably imperfect realities and an unimpeded perfection incapable of concrete actualization. (And there are different ideals precisely because goods are diverse and incommensurable; there are different values and different priorities among them that are always possible.) The useful work of an ideal is to serve as a goad to effort by preventing us from resting complacently satisfied with the unhappy compromises demanded by the harsh realities of a difficult world.

Ideals originate in the use of imagination to contemplate value possibilities that transcend the restrictive confines of the real. This transcendent aspect of ideals—their inherent "unrealism"—clearly poses problems of rational legitimation, particularly so in view of the present account of rationality in terms of optimization. We must confront the argument:

- Rationality is a matter of optimization, of doing "the best we can."
- Ideals outrun the limits of practicable achievability—of "what we can do."

Therefore: Ideals conflict with rationality.

This sort of objection to ideals as inherently irrational must be addressed, and we shall return to it in due course. First, however, a word about the optimism at issue with a commitment to ideals.

IV

Optimism And Pessimism

On the Pragmatic Power of Expectations

Synopsis

(1) The quarrel between an optimistic and a pessimistic appraisal of the world's course is an ancient one. (2) But there are very different sorts of optimism, and distinct constructions of the theory must be considered. (3) There are several variations of present-condition optimism. (4) Also, meliorism or progressivism has many forms. All of them are difficult to substantiate, though also difficult to refute. (5) Attitudinal optimism, an optimism of evaluative outlook rather than predictive belief, is an interesting variant of the position. (6) It can be justified in various sorts of circumstances. (7) Pessimism also has many versions. (8) A pessimistic attitude is much harder to justify than an optimistic one—the circumstances in which it can engender useful consequences are few and far between. (9) A dedication to ideals represents a significant and interesting mode of optimism.

1. Modes of Optimism

The quarrel between optimism and pessimism has been raging since classical antiquity. Following the lead of the Socrates of Plato's *Timaeus,* the Stoics taught that the world's arrangements are designed for the best and promote the good of all.[1] The followers of Hegesias, on the other hand, maintained to the contrary that nature is intractable and makes the achievement of well-being (*eudaimonia*) impossible for man.[2]

Optimism pivots on the contention that things are well with the world, that the existence and nature of this world, as is, are on balance for the good. But such a general view can take very different specific forms, depending on whether it is maintained that the condition of things is

(1) (presently) in good order; or
(2) *tending* toward the good—that in the natural course of events, matters will ongoingly assume a better condition; or
(3) *moveable* toward the good—that matters can be impelled in this direction provided only that we do the right things to bring this about.

Three different questions are at issue: how things *are,* whither they *tend,* and what *opportunities* are open. When these questions are answered favorably, we may call the three resultant positions *actuality* optimism, *tendency* optimism, and *prospect* optimism, respectively.

Actuality optimism takes the stance that things stand in good condition—that, on the whole, all is right with the world in the prevailing order of things. Such a view is usually (but not nec-

[1]For a compact account of Stoicism, see P. P. Hallie, "Stoicism," in *The Encyclopedia of Philosophy,* ed. by P. Edwards (New York, 1967), 8:18–22. Regarding the Stoic metaphysics of nature, see S. Sambursky, *Physics of the Stoics* (New York, 1959).

[2]Diogenes Laertius, *Lives of the Philosophers,* 2, sect. 94.

essarily) bound up with commitment to the benevolence of a presiding deity. This view was already voiced by Plato, who maintained that "Since he judged that order was in every way for the better, God brought it [the world] from disorder into order" (*Timaeus,* 30A).

Tendency optimism, also called *meliorism,* is something very different from actuality optimism. It does not necessarily hold that all is well with the world as is; it simply takes the stance that things are getting better. It compares the present with the relevant future and envisions an improvement in the confident conviction that, whatever might be happening now, better times lie ahead. (However, since improvement as such is at issue, the change could in principle merely be a change from terrible to bad, rather than one from good to even better.)

Prospect optimism compares the present as it stands with the prospective future that our efforts and opportunities put at our disposal. It looks to the *presumably realizable* future and maintains that suitable actions on our part can pave the way to improvement. (By contrast, the belief that things will deteriorate despite our best efforts to the contrary, represents a prospect pessimism.) Both meliorism (tendency optimism) and prospect optimism are oriented toward the future. But tendency optimism holds matters *will* get better of their own accord, while prospect optimism holds they *can* get better if only we do the right things.

Optimism in all its forms is indissolubly linked to the dimension of value. All the various modes of optimism are *evaluative* positions that contemplate some manner of goodness:

- Actuality optimism: things *are* in good condition.
- Tendency optimism: things *are moving* toward the better.
- Prospect optimism: things *are moveable* toward the better.

Optimism as it is being considered here is a general position about "the state of things" at large. Of course, people also speak of "being optimistic" about the favorable outcome of a *partic-*

ular situation or episode—the expectation that all will turn out well in a particular case. Our present concern, however, is with *optimism* at the level of generality, rather than with the case of such episodic expectations with respect to individual outcomes. The single-case "optimism" of the gambler who, presumably in the face of much counterevidence, thinks that he is bound to win *this* time, or of the drunkard who thinks that *this* bottle will engender no unfortunate results, lies outside the range of the present discussion.

2. *Parameters of Optimism*

Four questions can be always raised with respect to any sort of optimism:

- *What things* are being held to be good/improving/improvable?
- *What manner* of "goodness" is at issue: *in what way* is something to be good or better?
- Just *how* good, or *how much* better?
- Good or better *for whom?*

These four questions reflect, respectively, the *range,* the *mode,* the *degree,* and the envisioned *beneficiaries* of the optimism at issue. By varying these factors, we can obtain, for example, such melioristic theses as: "The life expectancy of infants is getting somewhat longer," "Hospital patients are receiving ever more effective care," or "The quality of life is improving for citizens of technically advanced societies."[3]

Different kinds of optimism arise from variation in the four parameters. With respect to range and mode this is clear enough. The issue of beneficiaries in particular opens up much scope. We have the prospect that those at issue are:

[3] A *technological* optimism to the effect that modern science and technology will create the conditions of a new social order is very popular in the Soviet Union under the influence of Friedrich Engels. Compare Boris G. Kuznetsov, *Philosophy of Optimism* (Moscow: Progress Publishers, 1977), which, despite its title, is a garden with very few philosophical plants.

- me = oneself (egocentric optimism)
- we = our group (parochial optimism)
- many or most people (general optimism)
- everyone (universal optimism)

The relative inclusiveness of the group of contemplated beneficiaries will determine the scope or scale of the optimism at issue. Of course, the fact that we ourselves can plausibly see improved conditions in the light of *optimism* will hinge crucially on our stance toward the group of beneficiaries—in particular on the question of whether we can identify with them in taking their interests to heart. If the beneficiaries were people whom we wish ill, the prospect of improvement in their lot would hardly represent an optimistic view.

The degree-oriented question "*How much* good or better?" also leads to considerable variation. Consider the scale:

G^*: as good as can be
$G+$: very good
G: good
O: indifferent
B: bad
$B-$: very bad
B^*: as bad as can be

Given such a spectrum, there are bound to be substantially different varieties of optimism—and, in particular, very different sorts of meliorism. A movement from G to G^* is one thing, one from B^* to B quite another. It is tempting to think that optimism is a matter of going "from good to better," and pessimism one of going "from bad to worse." But this is a grave oversimplification that takes one prominent case as representative of the whole.

Again, optimism is sometimes characterized as the view that "good will ultimately prevail over evil." But this too is a very

Display 5 A HYPOTHETICAL COURSE OF CHANGE

Group No.	*Average Initial Condition*	*Average Final Condition*
1	G−	G+
2	B	O
3	B*	B

special form of the doctrine. Consider a world populated by three groups, whose condition is viewed by a certain theory as subject to the course of change set out in Display 5. This theory is surely optimistic, since things are getting substantially better for all three groups. All the same, we do not have a condition where the good ultimately predominates: in the end, the majority of groups still occupies a condition other than good.

3. *Different Constructions of Actuality Optimism*

Let us examine actuality optimism somewhat more closely. Markedly diverse versions result with varying positions regarding the standing of the bad, seeing that one's view of *the status of negativity* will engender very different results:

(1) *Absolutistic optimism.* Everything is literally for the best. All negativity is only *seemingly* such. Anything bad is, even at worst, only a lack or imperfection—a shortfall of the good. Negativity (badness, evil) is nothing substantial as such; everything there is is good, though perhaps in varying degrees.

(2) *Instrumentalistic optimism.* There is actual negativity (badness, evil), but whenever present, it serves as a causal means to a greater good. There is always a chain of causes and effects through which any evil is ultimately productive of a predominating good. All those clouds have silver linings: any item of negativity is in fact a causally productive

means operating toward augmenting the good. The bads of the world are causally necessary conditions for the realization of greater goods.

(3) *Compensatory optimism.* There indeed is evil and negativity. And it is not always causally productive of a predominating good—not in every case simply a means causally conducive to a greater good in just exactly that same causal locality. But at the overall, collective level, the good outweighs the bad. The world is a systemic whole of interlocking elements, and matters are so arranged that a preponderant good always *compensates* for the presence of evil. The good and the bad stand in a relationship of *systemic interconnection:* evil is an integral and irremovable part of a holistic world order that embodies a greater good.

Quite different things are at issue here. With (1) we have a "blind" optimism that refuses to see negativity as something real. With (2) we have a theory of *causal facilitation* that acknowledges the reality of negativity but sees it as a means to greater good. With (3) we have a theory of *compensation* that sees negativity outweighed by a coordinated positivity in the world's overall systemic arrangements.

Some historical observations are in order. It would seem that (1) is not squarely held by any (Western) philosopher since the neo-Platonism of classical antiquity—apart from mystics and spiritualists.[4] The position is clearly at odds with the usual Christian view of the Fall of Man, and so to find its more common expression, we must turn to the Oriental religions, which see the phenomenal world with all its evils as *maya* or illusion. Voltaire's Dr. Pangloss, who sometimes talks in the manner of (1), comes closer to holding (2). But Leibniz, who sometimes talks in the instrumentalistic manner of (2), actually holds the

[4]Mary Baker Eddy wrote that "evil is but an illusion, and it has no real basis. Evil is a false belief." *Science and Health* (authorized edition, Boston, 1934), p. 480, sects. 23–24.

compensatory version at issue in (3). Accordingly, Voltaire's parody of the bad-will-lead-to-good idea in *Candide* does not really hit its target, Leibniz.

A theory that denies the existence of the bad only because it *also* denies the existence of the good within the context of a comprehensive denial of *all* value in the world's arrangements—in short, a Spinozistic negation of objective value—cannot be called a form of optimism. It falls outside the optimism-pessimism spectrum and is at odds with it.

4. *Tendency Optimism (Meliorism or Progressivism)*

Tendency optimism (meliorism) is not a single theory but a madding crowd of theories of the most diverse kinds, with little in common save their generic structure: things of some sort are getting better in some way or other for certain beneficiaries. In particular, when these beneficiaries are people-in-general, then a melioristic position represents a doctrine that sees the world's arrangements as fundamentally favorable to the interests of man.

Meliorism in all of its versions constitutes a *substantive* doctrine about the nature of the world and its course of events. Once a standard of good and bad is given, it represents a factual thesis to the effect that a course of change of a certain sort is under way and is, accordingly, matter-of-factly true or false. This is illustrated by what is perhaps the most usual and familiar form of meliorism, that based on the following parameters:

- range: conditions of life ("quality of life")
- mode: qualitative improvement
- degree: from bad (B) to very good ($G+$)
- beneficiaries: mankind at large

The resulting melioristic thesis maintains that the quality of life is getting ever better for people at large and is moving toward a generally good condition. Once we are informed about how this matter of "quality of life" is to be assessed, the thesis becomes a straightforward factual one that turns on how matters actually stand.

But while such a melioristic view is clearly factual in character, the fact at issue is patently an *evaluative* fact. Meliorative optimism stakes a claim that can be understood (and substantiated) only relative to a suitable standard of value to provide the necessary yardstick of evaluation. It is a substantive doctrine that is predicated on an essentially normative basis.

With any mode of meliorism, the question of the *pace* of improvement will always arise. When things are held to be getting better and better, the issue of velocity looms—a snail's pace vs. an avalanche-like rush. Moreover, any meliorism that looks to a coming improvement leaves open the question of just *when* this transformation will come about—whether soon or in the impenetrable fog of a future "eventually." If we look optimistically with Peirce to a cognitive victory of science over nature or with Marx to the political triumph of proletarian power, there yet remains the crucial issue of just when this happy eventuation is to be realized. With eschatological meliorism, as with doomsday theologies, that all-important question of timing is always there.

Meliorism is indissolubly linked to the idea of *progress*. Any theory of progress is a mode of meliorism—and, conversely, any meliorism a progressivism. For progress necessarily involves something more than mere *change*—namely, *improvement*. Progress has to involve change in some positively evaluated direction, encompassing a sequence of events in whose course things are "getting better" in some fashion or other. Accordingly, there will be as many distinct types of meliorism as there are types of progress. Very different sorts of "courses of ongoing improvement" can be contemplated: material, intellectual, social, moral progress, and the like.

The complexity and diversity of meliorism come to the fore in this connection. The same range of questions that apply to meliorism in general will apply to a progressivism of any sort: how fast, how far, how distributed, etc.

The distributional aspects of meliorism are of particular interest. Suppose a scale from 0–100, a *hedonic* scale, say, or a scale of *quality of life,* or some such—the details do not matter as long as we are operating in a context where "bigger is better." Consider now two very different situations:

Case 1: The *average* gets bigger and bigger, but the *minimum* gets ever less.

Year 1: 90% of the time at 90, 10% at 20
Year 2: 90% of the time at 95, 10% at 10
Year n: 90% of the time at halfway between the preceding year's 90% value and 100; 10% of the time at halfway between the preceding year's 10% value and 0.

Case 2: The *average* gets less and less, but the *minimum* gets ever bigger.

Year 1: 90% of the time at 90, 10% at 10
Year 2: 90% of the time at 70, 10% at 20
Year n: 90% of the time at halfway between the preceding year's 90% value and 50; 10% of the time at halfway between the preceding year's 10% value and 30.

These examples show that we will get a very different sort of "course of ever-continuing improvement" depending on whether we focus on the situation *on the average* or on the situation *at the minimum.*[5] There is a substantial prospect for disagreement and controversy with regard to just this question, "Does improvement in a particular respect actually constitute an improvement-on-the-whole?" With melioristic optimism, it may not be all that clear exactly what sorts of "course of im-

[5] Recall the comparably problematic position of John Rawls's *Theory of Justice* (Cambridge, Mass., 1971) that the demands of justice focus on the condition of those at the very bottom of the scale.

provement" should actually count as a *meaningful* or *significant* improvement. This question of an overall standard of improvement is a potentially complicated issue that must be resolved before a definitive version of meliorism is really at hand.

It is illuminating to consider the historical example of Leibniz in this connection. Leibnizian optimism is a complex and many-sided theory—a combination of several distinct forms of optimism. It involves, as we have seen, an endorsement of the compensatory version of actuality optimism. But another important feature is the contention that this world of ours is "the best possible world"—with stress on *possible*. There is, no doubt, a good deal that is not right with the world, but all the attainable alternatives are even worse. (Voltaire's ironic plaint, "Si c'est ici le meilleur des mondes possibles, que sont donc les autres?," implements rather than invalidates the Leibnizian approach.)

Leibniz was not one of those rosy-visioned theologians who argue that all of the world's evils and imperfections are mere illusions—that if only we saw things more fully and deeply, we would come to realize our mistake and reclassify all those negativities as goods. As they see it, all imperfection is only *seeming* imperfection—evils are simply shadows needed to secure the painting's overall effectiveness, and any complaint about the badness of things reflects a misunderstanding arising from an *incomplete* understanding.[6] But this possible (albeit problematic) line of absolutistic optimism just is not Leibniz's. Leibniz was quite prepared to recognize that much is wrong in the world. But all the other possibilities are worse. (Even a half full barrel can be fuller than all the rest.) Leibniz recognized evil as real. But he saw it as a systemically necessary condition for the greater good. The myth of Sextus at the end of the *Theodicée* illustrates this: "The crime of Sextus serves for great things: It renders Rome free; thence will arise a great empire, which will

[6]This is essentially the doctrine of Plotinus: all existence roots in the divine One and is therefore good. Evil is not something positive and real as such, but only something negative, a mere lack or deficiency of good. See especially *Enneads,* III, ii, 3–18; IV, iii, 13–18; IV, iv, 45; and passim.

show noble examples to mankind."[7] The world's arrangements are systemically interconnected. If we improved something here, even more would come unstruck over there—an "improvement" at one point of the system always has damaging repercussions at another.[8] (As with the harmony of a painting, however, the connections are matters of harmonization and systemic interlinkage, not of causal interaction.)

A further aspect of Leibnizian optimism is a meliorism with respect to the conditions of life for organic creatures in general and rational beings in particular. Of course, this is not to say that they are superbly good or (given the inherent imperfections of finite creatures) that they can ever become so. But things will improve on balance in the long run.

The salient feature of Leibniz's position remains in its commitment to a compensatory optimism that sees the world as good on the whole. It is *now and always* the case that, on balance, considering everything, the good outweighs the bad even here and now. Via the Christian neo-Platonism of thinkers like Augustine and Aquinas, Leibniz is deeply committed to the idea of a cosmic order that is essentially good. Good predominates over evil at every stage of the world's history. Leibniz sees this as essential to regarding the world as the creation of a benevolent deity. (In *this* regard, Schopenhauer's pessimism is a flat-out denial of Leibnizian optimism. Unlike Voltaire, Schopenhauer identifies his target correctly.) In any case, the example of Leibniz shows that a meliorism of the tendency-optimism variety is perfectly compatible with the endorsement of an actuality op-

[7] G. W. Leibniz, *Theodicée,* sect. 416.

[8] One recent author writes: "It is of course common knowledge that Leibniz believed that the appearance of evil in the world was only a symptom of our defective or limited understanding" (Catherine Wilson, "Leibnizian Optimism," *Journal of Philosophy* 80 [1983]: 765–83 [see p. 767]). But "common knowledge" is quite wrong here. Leibniz holds not that evil in the world is mere appearance but rather that it is compensated for by a preponderant good.

timism. Its improvability need not be seen as conflicting with the world's goodness as is.

Given this combination of views, there is no doubt that Leibniz's position is properly characterized as a version of optimism. But it is certainly not one of the facile ostrich-head-in-the-ground sort, which maintains that everything is just fine and sees no evil simply because it refuses, in a Pollyannaish fashion, to look evil in the face.

Is meliorism tenable at all? *Memento mori.* Does not the inevitability of death automatically preclude any possibility of being optimistic about the condition of man? Presumably not. The inexorability of death does indeed preclude the possibility of ever-continuing improvement at the level of the individual. But the general condition of the continuing group (clan, nation, species) may well improve, despite the merely transient presence of its particular members. ("I myself grow older," Caesar lamented, "yet the crowd in the Appian Way ever remains the same age.") Thus only the egocentric person who is concerned for himself alone is denied a recourse to optimism. Those whose wider range of concern embraces their posterity at large can in principle be optimistic about the human condition—ignoring for the moment such remote eventualities as the "heat death" of the solar system.

On the other hand, it would seem that mainstream Christianity is at odds with an unalloyed optimism regarding the condition of man as such. The kingdom it contemplates is not of this world, and it is not through their own powers and abilities that men can come to enter it. The progressivistic theory of the perfectability of man is a modern notion through which theorists of the Age of Enlightenment sought to supplant an older, less sanguine view of human prospects here on earth.

In any case, the melioristic thesis that things are tending toward the better is generally difficult to establish. The best we can standardly claim on *evidential* grounds is that things are getting better *at present.* And this seldom affords a firm guarantee for the future. (Our most secure inductive conclusion is that the long-term projection of current tendencies is generally inappropriate.)

The fact that meliorism is hard to substantiate has its other side in the fact that it is also hard to refute. Even if things have not gone well of late, this may well be a matter of preparation for a strong spurt toward the better: *reculer pour mieux sauter.* Sometimes one must travel east to go west—via the Panama Canal, for example. Appearances can be deceiving; the circumstance that things do not look to be getting better does not really mean they are not. The fact that melioristic optimism is hard to refute on evidential grounds opens the door to contemplating its acceptance on a nonevidential basis through a pragmatic rather than probative route to validation. This idea has important ramifications.

5. Attitudinal Optimism

As we have so far considered it, optimism is a *substantive* and factual (albeit value-determined) position. But there is room for yet another version—an optimism whose character is *attitudinal* rather than strictly *factual.* It is represented by a policy of proceeding (when possible) in the confident hope that a future-oriented optimism of tendency or prospect is indeed warranted—that things will work out well and matters continue to improve. Such attitudinal optimism is something very different from the descriptively factual modes of optimism with which we have dealt so far. It does not presuppose the actuality of a meliorative tendency or prospect. Rather, it is an attitudinal disposition toward viewing things in a favorable light as a basis for action. Attitudinal optimism is not a matter of a cognitively based conviction regarding how things will comport themselves in the world, but represents a praxis-geared posture of hopeful belief. What is at issue is not a well-evidentiated *thesis* but a *hopeful attitude* one takes toward the future when this is not precluded by the state of our information.

The assumption of such a position accordingly involves no actual *prediction* that the contemplated course of improvement will eventuate but only a *confidently hopeful anticipation* that this will occur. Unlike doctrinal optimism, attitudinal optimism is not a matter of predictive foreknowledge so much as hopeful expectation in the absence of contrary information. It inserts itself into the gaps that arise where the established facts are insufficient or indecisive, neither resting on the facts of the matter, nor defying them. What is at issue is a point of practical policy rather than one of factual foreknowledge.

Hegel was an optimist, and the fundamental optimism of their master is shared alike by the Hegelian left and the Hegelian right, but in very different ways. On the left lies the tendency optimism represented by the eschatological posture of dialectical materialism—a melioristic view predicated on the historical inevitability of a better order of things (for the proletariat at any rate). And on the right lies the attitudinal optimism of the German idealists—a position that is not comparably eschatological but represents an optimism of attitude and intellectual orientation rather than historical process. The former is an essentially predictive position, the latter an essentially attitudinal one.

Many expressions of attitudinal optimism are of course to be found in the pragmatic philosophy of William James, but its main theoretical exponent is the obscure Austrian philosopher Hieronymus Lorm.[9] With an eye on Kant's distinction between a phenomenal and a noumenal order, Lorm contrasts the order of experience (*Erfahrung*) with the order of sensibility (*Empfindung*). The bitter lessons of experience endorse pessimism, but the positive inclination of human sensibility calls for a life-

[9] See Hieronymus Lorm, *Der grundlose Optimismus: Ein Buch der Betrachtung* (Vienna, 1894). Ueberweg's *Grundriss* (pt. IV, 12th ed., Berlin, 1923), provides some information about this author.

enhancing optimism. Lorm accordingly endorses an attitudinal optimism (*Meinungs-Optimismus*) that is evidentially "groundless," because it flies in the face of our actual experience of how the world actually goes (our *Erfahrungs-Pessimismus*). But it is nevertheless seen as valid—experience to the contrary notwithstanding—as an expression of the inner spirit of man. As in Kant, we are dual citizens belonging both to an empirical realm where optimism is inappropriate and to a noumenal realm where optimism is mandatory.

Attitudinal optimism is thus a matter of outlook and perception—or attitude rather than expectation. The tendency optimist counsels *patience:* "Wait! Things will get better." The attitudinal optimist counsels *confidence:* "Hope! Don't let your spirit be crushed by present adversity. Spirit is something too valuable to be diminished by events whose overall worth in the larger scheme of things isn't all that big." Attitudinal optimism accordingly represents a fundamentally *evaluative* rather than a factually *predictive* posture.

6. *Validating Attitudinal Optimism*

But can these positions of personal attitude and empirical fact be kept apart? Does the rational validation of an optimistic attitude not presuppose a melioristic stance? Does *attitudinal* optimism not somehow require the support of optimism-warranting belief and thus require a grounding in scientific *foreknowledge?*

Not at all. It is perfectly possible for someone to adopt an optimistic attitude—quite reasonably and rationally—without establishing in advance the factual thesis that a substantively optimistic trend or tendency indeed obtains. Even in situations where one cannot evidentiate a melioristic tendency, one may well be able to validate an attitudinal optimism—not, to be sure, on evidential grounds but on pragmatic ones. One can, that is, validate attitudinal optimism by maintaining (1) that factually *nihil obstat,* that the factual evidence does not stand in its way in that no preclusive counterindications are at hand, and (2) that positive consequences will (or are likely to) follow upon my proceeding in a hope-and-expectation of optimistic tenor. These considerations yield a pragmatic rather than evidential justification—a justification on the basis of *consequences* rather than *grounds*. Accordingly, I can (quite reasonably) proceed to plan and conduct my actions in the firm hope that a favorable course of developments will unfold without first determining that this is actually (or indeed even probably) the case.

Consider an example. When the objective facts do not forbid it, am I entitled to take an optimistic attitude about the nation's recovery from a condition of economic slump and recession? A question of this sort can be addressed as an issue of *practical* (rather than *evidential*) reasoning. As such, it can be viewed in the light of the standard and established decision-theoretic method of choice resolution on the basis of expectations as depicted in Display 6.

Which alternative has the bigger expected value? On standard decision-theoretic principles, the top alternative is to be chosen (or not) accordingly as its "expected value" (the sum of its outcome values multiplied by their respective probabilities) exceeds that of its rival. This condition comes down to

$$px + (1 - p)y \gtrless (1 - p)u + pv$$

or equivalently

$$p([x - v] + [u - y]) \gtrless u - y$$

Accordingly, what matters for adopting the top alternative is not that p be *large* as such, but simply that it be larger than a suitable quantity determined by the particular relationship of those various outcome values (x, y, u, v).

For example, suppose that $x = v + a$ and $y = u + a$ with $a > 0$—reflecting that there is a certain added positivity due

Display 6 THE EXPECTED VALUE OF OPTIMISM

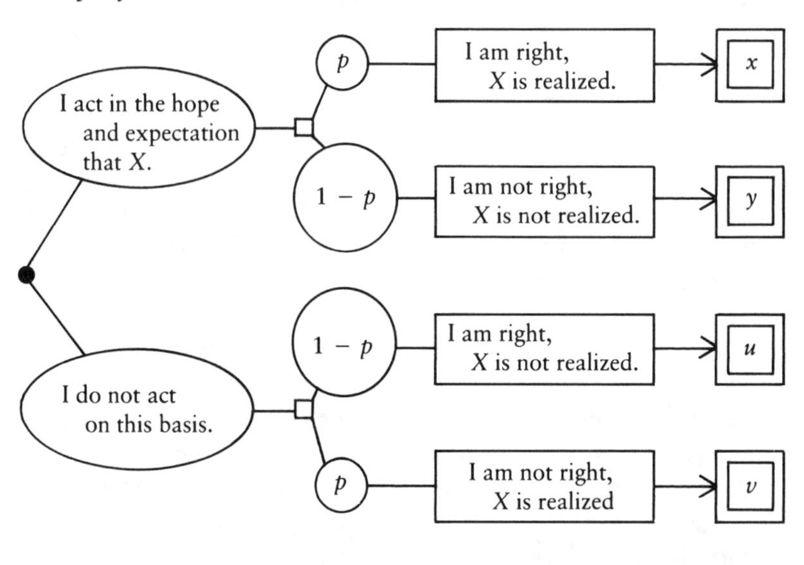

simply to acting in the hope and expectation that x, regardless of how matters ultimately turn out. In this particular case, the choice-determining inequality becomes

$$p(a - a) \gtrless - a$$

which—regardless of the particular value of p—is automatically resolved in favor of the top alternative, exactly as we should expect in the indicated circumstances. The example envisions a (perfectly feasible) situation where optimistic action simply *dominates* its alternative because it yields a preferable result no matter how things turn out.

Again, consider a rather different sort of case, one in which one's actions and efforts affect not the outcomes as such but the probabilities of realizing them, as per Display 7. Here we shall suppose that $p > p'$—that optimistic action increases the pros-

Display 7 A SPECIAL CASE

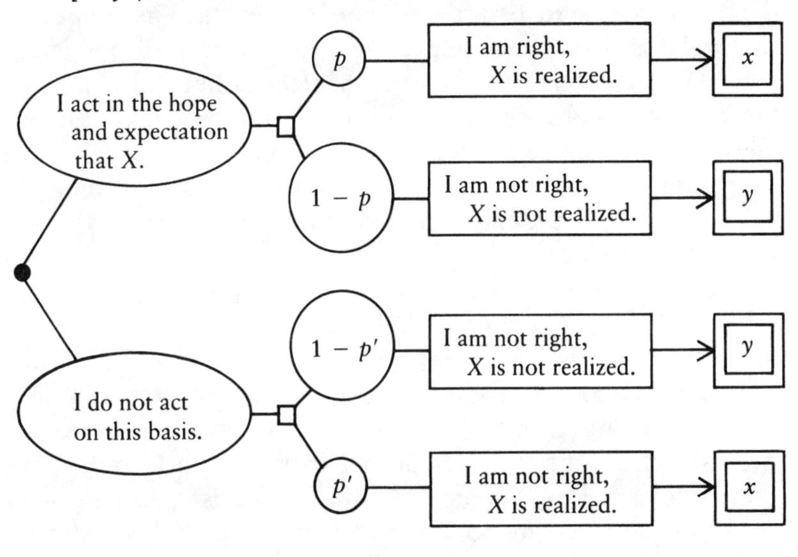

pects of a favorable outcome by some quantity, however small. The choice-determinative relationship is now

$$px + (1 - p)y \gtreqless (1 - p')y + p'x$$

or equivalently

$$p\,(x - y) \gtreqless p'(x - y)$$

As long as $x > y$—as long as that hoped-for outcome is indeed favorable—the top alternative automatically prevails, irrespective of the size of p. The principle at issue here is not that of the precept "Proceed in good hope and you will (certainly or at least very likely) succeed," nor yet that of the precept "Proceed in good hope since you have nothing to lose thereby," but rather that of the precept "Proceed in good hope and you will improve the chances of a success." If a policy for guiding one's actions can make even a small positive contribution to the probability that a desirable state of affairs will be realized, then its adoption can make good rational sense. When the balance of potential advantage is favorably adjusted, then those hopeful expectations are rationally defensible—albeit in the pragmatic rather than evidential mode of rationality.[10]

Yet how is one to reply to the objector who says: "Attitudinal optimism is not rationally justified in the absence of evidential support. In such cases one should not form anticipations at all but simply await developments." The response is straightforward. *Why not* adopt such a posture? Why simply wait with folded hands rather than act in hopeful expectation—particularly if such action can serve to improve the prospects of a favorable outcome?

This decision-theoretic perspective carries us back to the position advocated by William James in *Pragmatism*. As long as I am appropriately convinced that a policy of hopeful action can make a positive difference, attitudinal optimism can make good decision-theoretic sense—even where factual determinations are infeasible. An optimistic attitude can manifest "the power of positive thinking," as per the example: "In the ordinary affairs of life, act (in the absence of evidence to the contrary) as if the people with whom you deal were trustworthy and honest." The justification of such a "pragmatic belief" can reside in the efficacy of the practical policy that it underwrites—its capacity to engender positive results—and need not call for preestablishing its substantive correctness as a factual thesis. It can, in principle, make perfectly good practical sense to proceed in a spirit of optimism even when the prospects of success are small. When we must play a stronger team, we do well to strive with an effort bolstered by sanguine hope, remembering that with luck even puny David can prevail over mighty Goliath and that victory is not invariably on the side of the big battalions.

[10] On the issues involved in the contrast between evidential and pragmatic justification, compare the author's book, *Pascal's Wager* (Notre Dame, 1985).

To be sure, this pragmatic justification of optimism is not general and universal. It encompasses only a particular range of cases—those in which there indeed is good reason to think that a policy of action on the basis of good hope and expectation may well pay off. It envisions a defense of optimism not in *all* circumstances but in *suitable* circumstances.

Consider the objection:

> Surely it is not rational ever to let our attitudes be shaped in a way that outruns the reaches of our knowledge. To allow our outlook to be influenced by our values is just a matter of inappropriate wishful thinking.

This objection hits wide of the mark in its insistence in the name of "rationality" that attitudes must be shaped by *knowledge* alone. Rationality is a matter of the intelligent pursuit of appropriate objectives. And here knowledge does not have it all to itself. Man is not a *purely* cognitive creature—we do not live by information alone and knowledge is not our only value. The sphere of our praxis must be allowed to play its part in the overall rational order of things. An optimistic attitude can thus be perfectly "rational" in appropriate circumstances.

There are two very different sorts of rationally valid expectations about the future—namely, *cognitively justified anticipations* based on evidence, and *pragmatically justified hopes* based on decision-theoretical considerations. The two can get out of step with one another. But there is nothing whatsoever irrational or unreasonable about this—when the decision-theoretic aspects of the issue are heeded, it makes perfectly good rational sense because quite different things are at issue. Cognitive rationality is not the only sort; practical rationality can also come into operation.

We face a fundamental contrast. Our anticipations of the future are factual. As such, they must reflect the facts as we assess them evidentially with reference to the data. But our warranted attitudes can be practical. As such, they can reflect our appropriate hopes as we assess them pragmatically with reference to their potential consequences. This difference paves the way for a wholly different approach at these two levels.

Acting so as to fly in the face of established *facts* is never rationally justified. But to fly in the face of mere *probabilities* can on occasion be justifiable. Indeed that is exactly what we standardly do in decision theory when we balance probabilities against prospective gains and losses, placing our bets on the side of the more favorable expectations. We can, quite appropriately, sometimes bet on long shots.

Even if I am pessimistic and believe that the chances of realizing the good are low no matter what I do, the fact remains that when these chances are increased by my taking an optimistic attitude, then I am well advised to do so. And this is the crux. Even for a pessimist, an optimistic attitude may well pay off.

To be sure, attitudinal optimism is not *necessarily* advantageous. In cases where optimism is indeed unwarranted—where things are in fact on a downhill course—it may well prevent one from taking proper safety measures, such as fleeing in the face of impending doom. (Similarly, pessimism can be disastrous if it prevents one from seizing potentially advantageous opportunities because one sees one's efforts as bound to be unavailing.)

The advantageousness, and thus the rational advisability of optimism or pessimism, will very much depend on conditions and circumstances. There are certainly situations in which optimism is unwarranted and where it is a matter of unrealistically inappropriate wishful thinking that verges on self-deception to persist in thinking that matters will eventuate favorably. It is clearly foolish to be optimistic in cases where a failure to cut one's losses is simply to throw good money after bad; attitudinal optimism would obviously be ill-advised here. The sensible thing is to control our attitudes by a rational analysis of the objective situation, including a realistic appraisal of both the likelihoods of possible outcomes and their potential costs and benefits. The course of wisdom is a guarded optimism, chastened by a realistic appreciation of the determinable facts.

The rational optimist is accordingly one who adopts this policy not as a *general rule* but as a *working presumption:* "In the absence of sufficiently powerful indications to the contrary, act in the confident hope that your efforts will prove to good avail." (What is at issue is a presumption on the same order as that which underlies trusting other people and believing what they say.) The sensible thing is not to be optimistic always and everywhere, in season and out of season, but to be discriminating and allow the characteristics of particular cases and circumstances their just due. From the rational point of view, attitudinal optimism is a policy whose appropriateness is not universal but limited.

7. *Pessimism*

Much of what has here been said about optimism has its counterpart on the other side of the coin, the side of pessimism.

In particular, pejorism is the reverse of meliorism, embodied in the claim that things are getting worse and worse. As such, it is not necessarily a matter of gloom and doom. In theory, the deterioration at issue may simply take us from superb to excellent.

Schopenhauerian pessimism, on the other hand, is the doctrine that, on balance, the world's evils outweigh its benefits—that the condition of sentient beings in general and intelligent beings in particular is such that pain exceeds pleasure and suffering outweighs happiness.[11] As Schopenhauer put it in characteristically picturesque language: "If you try to imagine, as nearly as you can, how much of misery, pain, and suffering of

[11] Schopenhauer, of course, did not invent this view. It was already urged against Leibniz by Voltaire (in *Candide*), by Maupertuis (*Oeuvres* [Paris, 1756], 1: 202–205), and by Kant.

every kind the sun shines upon in its course, you will admit that it would be much better if the sun had been as little able on the earth as on the moon to call forth the phenomenon of life, and if here, as there, the surface were still in a crystalline state."[12] Even in such a view, however, it does not necessarily follow that it would be better if the world did not exist at all. For it is possible to take the line that benefits in the nonaffective range (including, for example, knowledge) could redeem an overall negative balance in specifically affective regards—that suffering is the price we pay for the realization of other values such as wisdom, and that it is worth it.

The fact that there are many different modes of optimism and pessimism means that it is possible to combine versions of the one with versions of the other. An interesting example is provided in the curious synthesis of Hegel and Schopenhauer (strange bedfellows!) that is presented in Eduard von Hartmann's *Philosophy of the Unconscious* (*Philosophie des Unbewussten,* 1869). He held, with Hegel, that there is indeed a spiritual dialectical progress in the evolution of consciousness and thought. But he also maintained, with Schopenhauer, that this is achieved at so great a cost in misery and suffering that it would be better if the world did not exist at all. (Similarly, Friedrich Engels was inspired by Malthus and Darwin to think of world history as the sphere of operation of a cruel force that exacts the sacrifice of millions of lives for the realization of every step of progress—a view that doubtless provided succeeding communist rulers with aid and comfort.[13])

Moreover, optimism and pessimism do not exhaust the field.

[12] A. Schopenhauer, "Nachträge zur Lehre vom Leiden der Welt," sect. 156.

[13] John Stuart Mill too wondered whether evolutionary progress was "worth purchasing by the sufferings and wasted lives of entire geological periods" (J. S. Mill, *Three Essays on Religion* [New York, 1874; reprint, New York, 1970], pp. 192–93). He eventually came to abandon the utilitarians' faith in progress and hoped at best for a steady-state condition in regard to human well-being. (See Lewis S. Feuer, "John Stuart Mill as a Sociologist," in J. M. Robson and M. Laine, eds., *James and John Stuart Mill: Papers of the Centenary Conference* [Toronto, 1976], pp. 98–99.)

Display 8 THE SPECTRUM OF POSITIONS REGARDING VALUE IN NATURE

1. Value (good and bad) does not apply to the world at all. (Spinoza, rigid materialism, positivism)
2. Value does indeed apply to the world and does so in such a way that
   (a) the world is maximally good—as good as it is possible for a world to be. (Leibniz)
   (b) the world is predominantly (though not maximally) good. (neo-Platonism)
   (c) the world is a (more or less) evenly balanced mixture of good and bad. (Manicheanism)
   (d) the world is predominantly (though not maximally) bad. (Schopenhauer)
   (e) the world is maximally bad. (Julius Bahnsen)*

*For this obscure German philosopher, see Rudolf Eisler, *Handwörterbuch der Philosophie* (Berlin, 1922; 2nd ed.), art. "Pessimismus," pp. 473–74. Bahnsen's principal work is *Der Widerspruch im Wissen und Wesen der Welt* (2 vols., Leipzig, 1882). His bibliography is given in Friedrich Ueberweg's *Grundriss der Geschichte der Philosophie,* 12th ed., rev. by T. K. Oesterreich (Berlin, 1923), 4: 341–42 and 701. For Bahnsen, the world is so designed as to frustrate every human hope and aspiration, and life is like a game of chance played against a diabolical house that is sure to win in the end. Death is not only the end of life but its *telos* as well. Life-affirmation is the worst policy: the more we bet on life, the larger our losses are bound to be. The precept "seek everywhere and choose the smallest evil, never the greatest good" is the course of true wisdom (*Der Widerspruch,* 2: 492).

There is, of course, also room for a Spinozistic naturalism that sees the world's course of events as totally indifferent to the affairs of man, inclined neither positively nor negatively toward matters of human good and evil, and providing a neutral stage-setting where matters of human well-being or ill-being are nowise programmed into the course of events as such but determined substantially by man himself.

And so, as Display 8 shows, every possible position in this domain has in fact been advocated by some thinker or other. As is often the case with philosophical controversies, every feasible alternative has found its exponent. (Of course, to note that a case has been made for each of these diverse alternatives is not to say that all are equally good.)

8. Pessimism versus Optimism

Pessimism invites despair, optimism confidence. The former looks on the dark side, the latter on the bright. Common sense and "realism" alike require us to recognize both dimensions—the question is one of where we focus, of what to accentuate. Optimism takes a characteristic stance here. It is a policy that goes beyond realism to enclose a principle of hope. It recognizes man as a creature of a Pascalian duality of mind and heart—of a binocular vision that sees with the body's eye what there is and with the mind's eye what there should be. It presses beyond fact to the impetus of value—not by failing to see things as they are but by looking also toward what there might and should be. As the optimist sees it, the good outweighs the bad not in the balance of actuality but in the balance of importance. He does not shut his eyes to the imperfections of the real but works in cheerful hopefulness toward their amelioration.

The risk of disappointment is the unavoidable price for the potential advantages of attitudinal optimism. If one is erroneously optimistic during a course of deterioration, one is going to find one's hopes dashed, one's expectations disappointed. Pessimism manifests the other side of the coin here. If one is a pessimist during a course of improvement, one is going to be pleasantly surprised when those unhappy apprehensions turn out to be unwarranted. To say this is not, however, to say that pessimism is a wise policy during times of betterment, for it is bound to lead one to lose out on opportunities. Moreover, the pessimist who resorts to this "pleasant surprise" line of thought to support his position runs into problems. For to justify taking a pessimistic stance on *this* basis—because one expects it to lead to pleasant surprises—is ultimately incoherent and inconsistent: it predicates pessimism on optimism. (The self-consistent line is for the pessimist, expecting deterioration, to support his position on grounds of its averting disappointment.)

Under what sorts of circumstances would an attitudinal pessimism that operates in the expectation that things are getting worse possibly be pragmatically justified as somehow useful or productive? Only if it actually helped us to prepare for the worst, to safeguard ourselves helpfully against difficulties that do indeed lie ahead. Thus attitudinal pessimism might pay off as a practical policy in leading people to take sensible precautions in the face of impending misfortune. But of course this can prove to good avail only if (factually speaking) those pessimistic expectations correctly characterize the objective situation. For pessimism to prove advantageous, the expectation at issue must be *correct*—the deterioration we anticipate must in fact be forthcoming.

In this regard, then, there is an interesting asymmetry between the two positions of attitudinal optimism and pessimism. A pessimistic attitude is of advantage only if pessimism is correct as a substantive position and things are indeed going downhill, while an optimistic attitude *can* also be useful when the reverse of its expectations is the case. The advantage of optimism is that it need not be predictively warranted to be pragmatically useful. Even if it eventuates as not justified in actual historical fact, attitudinal optimism can induce us to make things better than they otherwise would be. This sort of thing cannot happen with attitudinal pessimism.

The optimist hopes; even when things look bleak, he anticipates a happy issue. The pessimist fears; even when there are good prospects of a favorable issue, he anticipates the worst and expects disaster. But fear is almost always a bad counsellor. Hope is seldom so. (Though it *sometimes* can be: the investor who expects that current stock rally to last forever is a fool.)

An optimistic attitude impels its owner-operator to act with confidence—to run risks in hopeful expectancy that things will go well. It supports activity and enterprise. A pessimistic attitude tends to immobilize. If one confidently expects the worse (or worst), there is little point save in safeguards and insurance. And a sufficiently deep pessimism will dissuade one even from taking such measures because one expects that even they will prove unavailing. Insofar as these attitudinal matters lie within our control, we do well to favor the optimistic approach. Hope invites the penalty of disappointment but has the benefit of sustaining courage in the face of adversity. Pessimism invites inaction and, even worse, a despair that brings no benefits at all. We prefer optimism to pessimism in our companions because optimism is by its very nature life-enhancing.

Little is more bleak and more inhumane than a life not actuated by some hope of better things to come—if not for oneself and one's posterity, then for one's successors at large. Concern for our fellows and our species is not altogether unselfish. By taking such a stance we enlarge our stake in the world's affairs and broaden the basis of that hopefulness that endows our own life and labors with a significance it would otherwise lack. The extinction of hope is the ultimate evil.

9. *The Link with Idealism*

These deliberations regarding the justification of an optimistic attitude have an important bearing on idealism. The person dedicated to an ideal presumably recognizes full well that he will not bring those idealized arrangements to concrete actualization. Yet his idealism can—quite appropriately—form the focus of an optimistic attitude, an attitude of hopeful expectation that action in the light of this ideal is appropriate and worthwhile. Such an attitudinal stance of an inherently optimistic nature should—and, in appropriate circumstances, can—be justified by arguing that action predicated on a hope and expectation of good success will lead to better results than could possibly be achieved by proceeding on the basis of more "realistic" expectations. (This aspect of ideals sets a theme to which we shall return in the concluding chapter.)

V

Ideals And Their Limitations

On the Need to Coordinate Our Ideals

Synopsis

(1) Ideals always involve the element of unattainable idealization; they envision a condition of affairs in which some value is realized in preeminent and thus "unrealistic" degree. (2) Ideals serve as guideposts to orient our deliberations about the appropriateness of actions—they both guide and energize our practical endeavors. (3) However, ideals can also "get out of line" when one element of a complex of values is aggrandized at the cost of the very life of others. In the realm of ideals, too, there must be a harmony of mutual adjustment and coordination. (4) Accordingly, a realistic compromise between various ideals is desirable and involves no "betrayal" of ideals.

1. *On Idealization*

An *ideal* represents an "idealized" view of things—a *vision* of sorts, a mind's-eye picture of a utopian condition of affairs in which the realization of certain values is fulfilled and perfected to reach "the height of imaginable perfection," as Rudolf Eisler's philosophical dictionary puts it.[1] Ideals are instruments of the imagination. They are fundamentally value oriented, abrogating "by hypothesis" certain limitations the real world imposes on the realization of value. Ideals serve as our index not of what *is* or *will* be, nor even of what *can* be, but of what *should* be. They represent a vision as to how things ought ("ideally") to stand in the world, even though they do not and indeed cannot do so.

The employment of *ideal* as a noun is relatively recent. Lessing informs us that it was first so used by the Italian Jesuit Francesco Lana (d. 1687).[2] The adjective *ideal* is older; we find it (as *idealis*) in use by Albert the Great (d. 1390),[3] and by later scholastics.[4] It is clearly related to one sense of the word *idea*—namely, its Platonic sense as an idealized exemplar (*paradeigmon,* that is, *idea prima* = *examplar primum seu archetypon*[5]).

The modern conception of an "ideal" was disseminated through the philosophy of Kant:

> But what I call the *ideal* seems even further removed from objective reality than the idea. By ideal I understand the idea not merely *in concreto* but also *in individuo,* as an individual thing determinable or even determined by the idea alone. . . . The ideal is therefore the archetype (*Urbild, prototypon*) of all things [of a given sort], all of which, as imperfect copies (*ectypa*) derive from it the substance of their possibility, and while

[1] Rudolf Eisler, *Handwörterbuch der Philosophie,* rev. ed. by R. Mueller-Freinenfels (Berlin, 1922), entry "Ideals." For a useful general account see also the article "Ideale" by Rudolf Malter in Hermann Krings et al., eds., *Handbuch philosophischer Grundbegriffe* (Munich, 1973), 3: 701–8.

[2] See Abraham Schlesinger, *Der Begriff des Ideals* (Leipzig, 1908), p. 2. Here, however, the name of this remarkable scientist and Leibniz-correspondent is misprinted as LARA.

[3] Rudolf Eucken, *Geschichte der Philosophischen Terminologie* (Leipzig, 1879), p. 68.

[4] In *Martianus Capella,* for example. See J. and W. Grimm, *Deutsches Wörterbuch* (1877), vol. 4, pt. 2, entry "Ideale."

[5] See Rudolf Goclenius, *Lexicon Philosophicum* (Frankfurt, 1613), 1: 209.

> approximating to it more or less, always fall infinitely short of actually attaining it.[6]

Three points come together in this Kantian conception of something ideal:

(1) being paradigmatic or archetypal
(2) being perfect and altogether flawless
(3) being unreal, imaginary, accessible in idea alone

As point (2) emphasizes, the factor of worth or value is a crucial component of the conception of the ideal. Ideals envision a condition of affairs in which some sort of value is realized in limitless and thus "unrealistic" degree.

The trio "liberty, equality, fraternity," which constituted political ideals for the ideologues of the French Revolution, illustrates the points of the preceding paragraph. Their devotees looked to a new order, where men, freed from the restrictive fetters of the ancient regime, would work together in cheerful cooperation for the common good. Hoping to overcome the deficiencies of the old order, they envisioned a transformation that could find no accommodation amid the harsh realities of an imperfect world.

The expression "ideally speaking" indicates a completeness without let or hindrance—a perfection that goes beyond anything actually realizable in this imperfect, sublunary dispensation. An ideal is a model or pattern of things too perfect for actual realization in this world. In this way, "ideally speaking" standardly contrasts with "speaking in the ordinary commonplace way." According to Cicero's *De republica,* Scipio affirmed that "though others may be called men, only those are truly men who are perfected in the arts appropriate to humanity."[7] It is

[6] Immanuel Kant, *C.Pu.R.*, A568–B506, A578–B606.
[7] Cicero, *De republica,* I, xviii, 28.

just this sort of contrast between the *real* and the *ideal* that is the basis of the idea of ideals.

There are, of course, very different types of ideals—personal, moral, political, social, religious, cognitive, aesthetic, and others. A taxonomy of ideals would be complicated indeed, seeing that there are bound to be as many different kinds of ideals as there are kinds of values. Even "purely theoretical" issues can have their ideal aspect, as is attested by the cognitive ideal of "perfected science"—a body of knowledge capable of answering our questions about nature in a way that satisfies such abstract desiderata as truth, comprehensiveness, coherence, elegance, and the other characteristic features of "the systemic ideal."

To be sure, one must distinguish between full-scale ideals and mini-ideals, between (1) something that is altogether and unqualifiedly perfect, and (2) something that is "as perfect as we can realistically expect to find," or "as perfect as is requisite for the immediate purpose at hand." It is the second, rather than the first, that is at issue in locutions like

- "That hammer is the ideal tool for the job."
- "She was an ideal wife for him."
- "Florida was an ideal locale for our midwinter vacation."

It is not this latter, qualified sort of ideality but the former, unqualified sort that will concern us here.

When we "idealize" in this stronger sense, we begin by considering some valued type of thing or state of affairs, characterized in functional, use- or role-oriented terms of being good *for* something. For example:

- a vacation: a period of time spent away from one's ordinary duties and dedicated to rest and relaxation
- a scientific theory: a thesis or hypothesis used to provide an explanatory account for some entity or process in nature

Idealization consists in envisioning an item of such a sort under the supposition that it plays the valued role at issue completely and perfectly without any limitation whatsoever: "a perfect vacation" or "a definitive scientific theory." The item at issue, the "ideal," is to be a perfect, complete, definitive instance of its type—a very model or paradigm that answers to the purposes at issue in a way that is flawless and incapable of being improved upon: "the true friend," "the flawless performer," "the consummate physician." Such ideals, of course, are "too good to be true."

We must accordingly reckon with the unrealism of our ideals. The ardent socialist who adopts economic equality as one of his ideals need not (and should not) expect it to be realized in full. He doubtless cannot even say just precisely what its concrete realization would actually be like. (For example, even if *X* and *Y* were fitted out with the same "goods and possessions," how could one make provision for their different tastes, needs, and capacities for enjoyment?) Again, suppose I were an ardent capitalist, who adopted free and unfettered competition as one of my cardinal ideals. The awkward fact remains that the production of some major goods, such as "public health" or "national security," just does not square with this model. There is something inherently unrealistic about our ideals: they are inherently incapable of "genuine fulfillment."

This aspect of "idealization" attaches to all ideals. It has important consequences, since it means that we cannot expect to meet with the realization of ideals in actual experience. The *object* at issue with an ideal (perfect democracy, definitive science, full realization of our own potential, etc.) cannot be brought to completed actualization in this world. Ideals are merely visions of things about which there is always an element of the visionary. In its very nature, "ideal" provides a *contrast* to "real": there is always some tincture of the imaginary about our ideals. They are not objects we encounter in the world; it is only through thought, and specifically through the *imagination,* that we gain access to the ideal.

2. *The Orienting Role of Ideals: Ideals as Useful Fictions*

What then is the ontological status of ideals?

Some theoreticians have viewed ideals as actually existing things. Plato, for example, thought they existed in a realm of their own. He conceded that ideals are not part of the world's furniture, and that they are accessible through thought alone. But he nevertheless viewed them as being *found* rather than *made* by minds—as self-subsisting objects existing in a separate, world-detached domain rather than as mere thought artifacts. In this way, various theorists maintain the self-sufficient existence of ideals, independent of the sphere of mind. But such a "realistic" view of ideals has its difficulties. Once we abandon Plato's view that ideals are causally operative in the world directly and immediately, independently of their role in human thought, we lose the basis for assigning them a thought-independent existence. The "reality" of an ideal lies not in its substantive realization in some separate domain but in its formative impetus upon human thought and action in this imperfect world.

The object at issue with an ideal does not, and cannot, *exist* as such. What does, however, exist, is the *idea* of such an object. Existing, as it must, in thought alone (in the manner appropriate to ideas), it exerts a powerful organizing and motivating influence on our thinking, providing at once a standard of appraisal and a stimulus to action.

As Kant saw the matter, an ideal is "a *regulative principle* of reason" that directs our minds to look upon the world *as if* certain "idealized" conditions could be realized—conditions that, as we full well recognize, are not and indeed cannot be actual.[8] They exist not as such but only in idea or imagination. All our ideals are idealizations imbued with an element of unrealism. The states of affairs they contemplate are mere fictions—mere thought pictures we cannot find actualized among

[8] Immanuel Kant, *C.Pu.R.*, A569–B597.

the real furnishings of this world. The objects they envision do not and cannot exist as such; they are *putative* objects akin to merely hypothetical possibilities. Like the perfected state of utopian theorists or the wise man of Stoic philosophy, an ideal is destined to remain outside the realm of the world's realities.

This view of the matter gets things substantially right. Ideals are best accommodated by an "idealism" that sees them as the products of mind (and mortal mind, at that).

The operation of ideals is accordingly confined to the domain of rational agents. Only mind-endowed intelligence can adopt guiding value ideals and act in their light, with a view to approximating such essentially fictive states of affairs. (This shows that "idealism" in the present sense is also linked to a metaphysical idealism that sees mind as playing a key formative role in shaping the world's arrangements.)

With the eyes of the body we see things as they are. With the mind's eye, we see them as they might and should be. (Imagination, that salient human resource, is crucial to the possession of ideals.) The discrepancy here can and should be not an occasion for discouragement but a goad to effort.

Ideals are in a way akin to such quasi-fictive reference devices as the equator or the prime meridian, which we do not actually encounter in physical embodiment on the world's stage. They are "navigation aids" as it were—thought constructions that we superimpose on the messy realities of this world to help us find our way about. The utility of an ideal lies in its capacity to guide evaluation and to direct action in productive ways. Ideals' crucial role is as a tool for intelligent planning of the conduct of life. To manage our own affairs satisfactorily—and to explain and understand how others manage theirs—we must exploit the guiding power of ideals.

By providing such bases of judgment, ideals serve to orient and structure our actions and give meaning and significance to our endeavors. They are guiding beacons across the landscape of life—distant, even unreachable points of reference that help us to find our way. We frequently should, generally can, and sometimes actually do design our own courses of action and evaluate those of others by using ideals as a reference standard.

For this reason, philosophers concerned with the elucidation of human goods and values find idealization useful. Time and again we see them resorting to such idealizations as

- the perfectly just man of Plato
- the perfectly wise man of the Stoics
- the ideal community of utopian political theorizing
- the social contract between ideally rational agents
- the perfection of inquiry in "ideal science" (Kant, Peirce)
- the "perfectly rational agent" of economic theorizing

In all such cases, we are confronted by an idealization invoked to explain and validate some major project of human endeavor.

To adopt an ideal is emphatically not to think its realization to be possible. We do (or should!) recognize from the start that ideals lie beyond the reach of practical attainability. Ideals accordingly do not constitute the concrete objectives of our practical endeavors but rather provide them with some generalized direction. Moreover, objectives are simply things we want and desire—for *whatever* reason. There is no suggestion that they are inherently valuable or worthy. But by their very nature ideals are held by their exponents to be objects of worth. An ideal of mine is not just something I want; it is a condition I am committed to considering as deserving of being sought. By their very nature, ideals are seen not as mere objects of desire (*desiderata*) but as desirable objects (*desideranda*): what counts with them is not what one finds that people do want but what one judges to be worthy of wanting.

A concrete objective is generally something realistic, a destination we think it possible to reach if only we try hard enough—a *terminus ad quem* toward whose realization we can strive. It corresponds to the top of Display 9. But it is *not* in this way of

Display 9

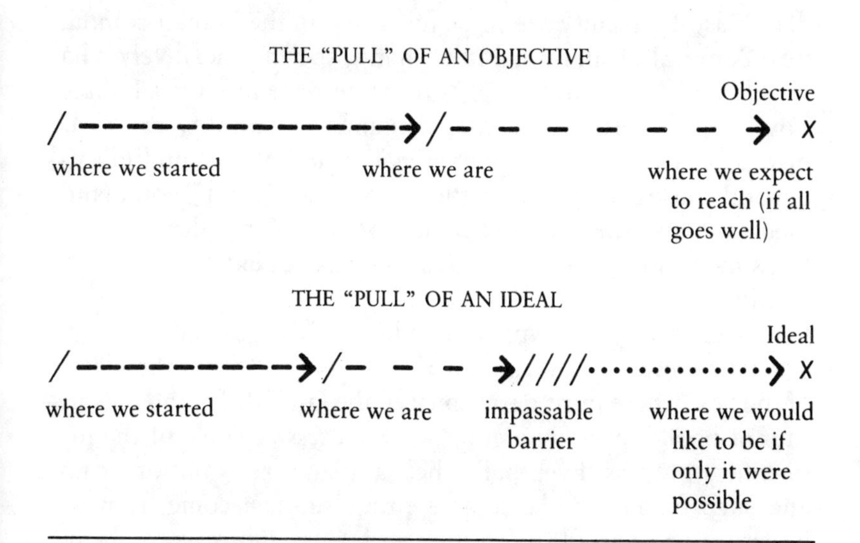

an attainable destination that an ideal provides us with "direction." Rather, the situation is something like that depicted at the bottom of Display 9.

We do not expect to attain the ideal, since we recognize full well that an impassable barrier separates us from its realization. But, miragelike, it beckons us onward. It does two things for us: (1) it does not let us rest content with simply staying where we are, and, still more importantly, (2) it furnishes us with guidance by orienting us in a direction in which to go. By doing this, ideals provide us with the guiding vision (however visionary!) of a better order of things. Preventing us from resting comfortably content with what it is we actually achieve, ideals lure us on, Siren-fashion, toward a better order of things—an order we are drawn to pursue unless we firmly bind ourselves, with Ulysses as precedent, to the mast of the world's realities. (Bitter experience tends to do this for us, which is why the old are generally less idealistic than the young.)

Ideals also differ importantly from norms. Take morality, for example. A moral norm specifies what *must* (or *must not*) be if violence to the moral order is to be avoided—i.e., if the *minimal* demands of morality are to be instituted in the human community. A moral ideal, on the other hand, specifies positively what *should* be if the moral order is to be perfected in a given direction—i.e., if certain *maximal* demands of morality are to be instituted. In the moral sphere ideals reach out beyond norms, beyond the *via negativa* of those "thou shalt not" commandments, toward the ampler demands of a utopian order of things. Thus moral ideals do not abrogate norms but extend or amplify them.

Our practical endeavors must ultimately be guided by the vision of an end beyond the practicable range. Behind the "letter of the law" there must be a "spirit of the law." Rules and reasons cannot prevail everywhere, at every successive stage of the justificatory process. Eventually their guidance runs out of steam, and such further guidance as we require must come from the illumination of an ideal. To stick with rules and reasons always and everywhere is actually inhumane. Their operation must function in a setting where there is some room for appeal "beyond the rules"—be it from commiseration, sympathy, kindness, or whatever—to some tempering influence from an idealized vision of human life. It is, after all, this sort of guiding vision that provides the rationale for the rules in the first place.

Ideals are generally particularized in some way—to a profession or craft, to a particular culture or nation ("the Roman ideal of citizenship"), and in principle even to a small group (a family) or perhaps even a single person (think of Sigmund Freud's "ego-ideal" and the whole issue of the sort of person we would ideally like to be—to try to make of ourselves).

If something is my ideal, I would certainly *welcome* others also seeing it in this light. But I cannot appropriately expect or demand it. Ideals lack the sort of universality we attribute to norms; there is something more particularized, more *parochial* about them. (The Greek and the Christian ideals of man differ significantly.)

The matter of *which* particular ideals people adopt admits of variation. Ideals, like goals, are relative to the particular values to which an agent subscribes, and to the priorities he gives them; they are not inherent in his status as a rational agent per se. A person who subscribes to certain ideals accordingly has no right to expect that others will do so as well, though he certainly does have a right to expect that they should respect his position.

Human goods are diverse. Different people with different personal experiences and dispositions have different priorities among values. And these can be incompatible. Your ideal state may emphasize liberty, mine order; your ideal lifestyle may require ongoing novelty, mine stability and regularity. Different people will have conflicting ideals. The ideal of a world-order where everyone's ideals can be accommodated is itself an ideal—and an emphatically unrealistic one at that.

People, of course, differ in their attachment to ideals—even as they differ in their attachment to other people, to material possessions, or to anything else. Some of us are pedestrians, inextricably engaged in the quotidian round of everyday concerns; others are high-flying visionaries, given to dreaming and scheming for a better day. Some are "realists" and view the human condition with contempt; others are "persons of high ideals," devoted to visions of the good, dedicated to a better condition of things, and given to expecting much—perhaps too much—of themselves and other people. But *this* sort of "realism/idealism" is a matter of mixture and proportion. Having *some* degree of involvement with values and ideals is part and parcel of being a normal human being. Man is an amphibious creature, constrained by the circumstances of his condition to operate in two realms, the real and the ideal—the domain of what is and the domain of what ought to be.

3. *The Pathology of Ideals*

All ideals involve the element of *idealization.* They represent putative aspects of excellence considered in isolation apart from other aspects. When we consider such values in separation from others, we engage in an act of *abstraction*—we put all other considerations aside for the time being. This, of course, is ultimately untenable—and so we have here another aspect of the "unrealism" of ideals. When thinking about an ideal, one should never forget these other considerations. To return to a previous example, a car's "safety" is a prime desideratum. But it would be foolish to contrive a "perfectly safe" car whose maximum speed is only 1.75 MPH. Safety, speed, efficiency, operating economy, breakdown avoidance, etc. are *all* prime desiderata of a car. Each *counts,* but none *predominates* in the sense that the rest should be sacrificed to it. They must all be combined and coordinated in a good car. The situation with respect to ideals is altogether parallel.

Ideals do not exist in a vacuum. They do not operate in isolation. They can be pursued only in a complex setting where other "complicating" factors are inevitably also present. Every individual ideal of ours must coexist alongside values within the context provided by an overall "economy" where every element must come to terms with the rest.

Two distinct points must be carefully distinguished. The first is the simple and essentially *economic* point that in a world of limited resources, we must make choices—we cannot have our cake and eat it too. This point is obvious (though not, to be sure, thereby unimportant). The second point, which is a more subtle one, is that the realities of the world are such that the pursuit of ideals is inherently limited by the inevitably *interactive* nature of things. With weight reduction, we increase the operating economy of a car at the sacrifice of its safety. Other things equal, one value factor is generally enhanced at the expense of another. In the political domain, for example, both public order and individual freedom are legitimate values. Yet the interests of the one can in general be advanced only at the cost of the other, lest liberty degenerate into a license to injure the interests of one's fellows. Different aspects of an "imperfect world" are at issue: in the one case, we have to do with man's limited resources. In the other, we are dealing with man's limited power, with the fact that even were our resources unlimited, there would nevertheless remain drastic, nature-imposed limits to the extent to which man's wish and will can be imposed on the realities of the world.

Ideals can be pursued only within *the limits of the possible* in a complex and no doubt imperfect world. In practice we have to content ourselves with subideal achievements. It is a key aspect of rationality—of ends-oriented intelligence—that it involves a coming to terms with this fact that considerations of "realism" must temper our dedication to ideals.

As Aristotle already observed, things can go awry through the neglect of due balance in the pursuit of perfectly sound and appropriate values. Family loyalty can engender nepotism, patriotism can inflate to jingoism, prudence can degenerate into avarice. And so the prospect of misbegotten ideals arises, whereby in the pursuit of some valued goals, one allows other values to be trodden under foot. The Nazi ideal of "racial purity" reflects such a misbegotten desideratum in which perfectly good values such as communal solidarity, pride in one's heritage, and group loyalty have overdeveloped into something monstrous, usurping the space created by abandoning other less parochial and more humane values.

Commitment to an ideal is inappropriate if it occasions the pursuit of values to become unbalanced. Here, as elsewhere, health is a question of harmony and balance—of giving the diverse elements of a rational economy of values a chance to flourish in their proper place. An ideal functions as simply one component within a system, which makes it possible to strike a reasonable balance between the different and potentially discordant values. The cultivation of ideals is profitable only within the setting of a concern for the overall "economy" of the system of values whose interaction imposes mutual constraints. And the health of such an economy is destroyed when one element is aggrandized by expanding its scope at the cost of the very life of others. Unreasonable dedication to an ideal is a dangerous thing. Public order is a great good. But when, like Robespierre, one sacrifices multitudes on its altar, things have gone too far. Like other powerful tools, ideals can be abused. Excesses are possible even—perhaps *especially*—in the pursuit of virtue.

"Sound ideals soundly pursued" is a good principle. Excellences that do not keep their proper place in an overall economy of values can metamorphose into horrors. Human stupidity and self-will can contaminate the pursuit of even sound values and noble ideals. The splendid ideals of the French Revolution led in a direct line to the Terror. Fanaticism results from the loss of any reasonable sense of what price is worth paying for advancing the realization of an ideal in terms of the sacrifice of other appropriate human values. It is not someone who is merely unprincipled who becomes a dangerous fanatic but someone whose dedication to an inherently proper ideal simply "gets out of hand."

To be sure, mere imbalance is not the worst prospect. For it is also possible for ideals to be outright bad—wicked, malign, and evil. The "values" they reflect can in principle include anti-values that look to a state of things that is far from good. Ideals are geared to values, and people can have inappropriate values. In this domain, as in others, they can be perverse. To be sure, this is not a light in which we can view our own ideals—any more than we can see our own goods as bads. But we ourselves are, of course, not the final arbiter.

Someone's ideals are no more necessarily valid than someone's values are necessarily valuable. People can (and do) prize things that do not *deserve* to be prized. What matters is thus not just that one has ideals but that one has sensible or appropriate ideals. And this is a matter of having ideals that conduce toward a life that is not only satisfying for its bearer but also worthy of respect from his fellows. The validity of ideals is a matter of so conducing our lives that we can take *both* pleasure *and* justifiable pride in them.

The person who lacks ideals is condemned to a bleak life, insufficiently warmed by the influence of values. But someone who adopts wicked ideals—or who pursues even benign ideals irrationally—is bound to prove a menace to himself and to others.

4. Realism versus a Betrayal of Ideals

The fact that our ideals and values limit one another in actual operation has important consequences. It means that while ideals *can*—nay *should*—be cultivated, they never deserve total dedication and absolute priority, because this would mean an unacceptable sacrifice of *other* ideals. Their pursuit must be conditioned by recognizing the existence of *a point of no advantage*, where going further would produce unacceptable sacrifices elsewhere, and thus prove counterproductive in the larger scheme of things.

In the pursuit of ideals, *unrealism* is thus the constant danger. There is an object lesson to be learned from the case of the man so intent on the cultivation of his pet ideal that he fails to realize that it may cease to be worthwhile when its pursuit blocks the way to other desiderata. Such unrealism is implicit in the pejorative connotation that an "idealistic" person is also naive in having an exaggerated and unrealistic view of the extent to which an ideal can actually be brought to realization without producing untoward "side effects."

Ideals are crucially important, but without an adequate realization of the realities and complexities of life, they are of little avail. By themselves, ideals are very *incomplete* guides to action.

Ideals aim at the superlative. When we contemplate the ideal state of something, we envision what is the very best of possible alternatives in this regard. And this is not enough for practical purposes. To apply any such principle in practice, we must know which of several feasible nonideal alternatives is to be preferred: we must not only know what is *the best* but also be in a position to determine which of several putative possibilities comes "closer to the ideal." (How far has the beginner come toward learning how to evaluate bridge hands when he is told that the perfect hand consists of the four aces, the four kings, the four queens, and a jack?) Ideals as such are oriented at a maximum. But in their cultivation it is the optimum of a balanced accommodation and harmonization that we must seek.

One must have both the "sensitive judgment" and the "practical know-how" needed to effect an appropriate working compromise among one's ideals. Ideals serve to point the way. But this does not resolve the practical choices that confront us in concrete situations. Having a destination is not much help: we must know about life's twists and turns as well. In and of themselves ideals are insufficient to provide the guidance we actually need.

The stress on ideals must accordingly be tempered by this recognition of the need to harmonize and balance values off against one another. In the realm of values, too, there must be a Leibnizian *harmonia rerum* where things are adjusted in an order of mutual compossibility.

The intelligent cultivation of an ideal requires us to realize that its pursuit can be overdone. Even as we can make the car so safe that we incur an unacceptable sacrifice of (say) its economy of operation, so we can emphasize individual liberty in the state to such a degree as to compromise public order, etc. Even in cultivating ideals there comes a point of counterproductiveness where "the better is the enemy of the good." An ideal whose pursuit in the prevailing circumstances cannot be carried on in a plausible and sensible way itself thereby becomes inappropriate in those circumstances.

A very important difference thus exists between a *compromise* of one's ideals and a *betrayal* of them.

Compromise occurs in the cultivation of an ideal when one tempers or limits its further pursuit because its interaction with other values requires some mutual accommodation—to press further with the supposedly "compromised" ideal in the prevailing circumstances would frustrate our other equally valid objectives. In this regard the compromise of ideals is inevitable, "realistic," and nowise reprehensible. Our "idealistic" dedication to ideals must be tempered by a "realistic" recognition that we must be prepared to settle for less—that our expectations can properly fall short of our aspirations. In all negotiations there is some element of compromise, and the pursuit of ideals proceeds amid a complex negotiation with the difficult circumstances of human life. There is nothing wrong with entering upon such a negotiation with substantial, perhaps inflated, demands. But if we are sensible, we shall do this in the full recognition that in this context, too, we must eventually "settle for less."

The *betrayal* of an ideal is something else again. It is a matter of sacrificing it for unworthy reasons: greed, convenience, conformity, or the like. To betray an ideal is to desist in its pursuit in circumstances where pressing on could well be productive. Betrayal involves *not going as far as one ought;* compromise, by contrast, involves *not going further than one ought.* The two things are very different.

The nature of compromise helps to explain how disagreement and discord can arise even between people who share an ideal in common. For when compromise becomes necessary, one can give different priorities to the several factors that are combined in a particular ideal. Even when we agree that a good state must afford its people *both* an orderly setting for their activities ("law and order") *and* freedom of action ("autonomy of choice"), we may well reach a parting of the ways when we confront situations where one of these desiderata must make way for the other.

VI

The Power Of Ideals

On the Role of Ideals as Instruments of Practice

Synopsis

(1) The serviceability of ideals derives from the fact that the character of our thought and action is directed and canalized by the way in which we look beyond the limits of the practicable. (2) Despite their fictional aspect, ideals become eminently useful instrumentalities through facilitating our pursuit of desirable ends. The worth and value of ideals lie not in their unattainable ideality but in their eminent utility—in their capacity to guide and facilitate the cultivation of values. (3) The absence of ideals is bound to impoverish a person or a society. (4) The legitimation of ideals is accordingly instrumental and pragmatic: they are valuable not for *their own* sake but for *ours* because of the good results they help us to realize.

1. The Service of Ideals

Ideals pivot about the question "If I could shape the world in my own way, how would I have it be?" And, of course, *every* voluntary action of ours is in its way a remaking of the world—

at any rate, a very small corner of it. To act intelligently is to act with due reference to the *direction* in which our own actions shift the course of things. And it is exactly here that ideals come into play. Our ideals guide and consolidate our commitment to virtues and moral excellences. Courage or unselfishness provides an example. Acts of courage or of selflessness often go beyond "the call of duty," exemplifying a dimension of morality that transcends the boundaries of obligation.

In an influential 1958 paper, J. O. Urmson stressed the ethical importance of the Christian conception of works of supererogation (*opera supererogationis*),[1] reemphasizing the traditional contrast between the *basic* morality of duties and the *higher* morality of preeminently creditable action "above and beyond the call of duty." Supererogation is accordingly best conceptualized not in terms of duty but in terms of dedication to an ideal. The values at issue are often symbolized in such "role models" as heroes and saints. An ethic of ideals can accommodate what is at issue here in ways in which a mere ethic of duty cannot.

These reminders of the limited range of a strictly deontological morality carry us back to Kant's ambivalent struggles with such particularly "meritorious actions" as risking one's own life to save others in a shipwreck. On the one hand, Kant views them as a danger rather than providing us with a model. For the example of noble or holy deeds can throw our moral sense off its proper course: "The mind is disposed to nothing but blatant moral fanaticism and exaggerated self-conceit by exhortations to actions as noble, sublime, and magnanimous."[2] On the other hand, Kant is unwilling simply to reject such behavior as morally inappropriate. And so he labors mightily to bring it within his duty-oriented framework, holding that, from the point of view of actual agent, a supererogatory act should in fact be seen as a duty—not, to be sure, one owed to the beneficiary as the

[1] J. O. Urmson, "Saints and Heroes," in *Essays in Moral Philosophy*, ed. A. I. Melden (Seattle, 1958). On this theme, see also David Heyd, *Supererogation: Its Status in Ethical Theory* (Cambridge, England, 1984).

[2] *C.Pr.R.*, p. 85 (*Akad.*).

individual he is but rather one owed to humanity as a whole.[3] But the artificiality of such a duty-geared reconceptualization of supererogation is only too clear. Nobody has a *duty* to his fellows to become a saint or hero; this just is not something we *owe* to people, be it singly or collectively. Such "duty" as there is will be that of "sense of duty"—an inner call to be or become a person of a certain sort. Here we are not, strictly speaking, dealing with a matter of duty at all but with a dedication to an ideal, the inner impetus to do one's utmost to make the world into a certain sort of place—perhaps only that small corner of it that consists of oneself.

A knowledge of their ideals gives us much insight into what people do. "By their ideals shall ye know them." We do know a great deal about someone when we know about his ideals—about his dreams, his heroes, and his utopias. The question of what gods he worships—power or fame or Mammon or Jehovah—does much to inform us about the sort of person we are dealing with. (To be sure, what we do not yet know is how *dedicated* he is to those ideals—how energetically and assiduously he puts them to work.)

Human aspiration is not restricted by the realities—neither by the realities of the present moment (from which our sense of future possibilities can free us), nor even by our view of realistic future prospects (from which our sense of the ideal possibilities can free us). Our judgment is not bounded by what *is,* nor by what *will* be, nor even by what *can* be. For there is always also our view of what *should* be. The vision of our mind's eye extends to circumstances beyond the limits of the possible. A proper appreciation of ideals calls for a recognition of man's unique dual citizenship in the worlds of the real and the ideal—a realm of facts and a realm of values.

It is remarkable that nature has managed to evolve a creature who aspires to more than nature can offer, who never totally feels at home in its province, but lives, to some extent, as an alien in a foreign land. All those who feel dissatisfied with the

[3] Compare the discussion in Heyd, *Supererogation,* p. 66.

existing scheme of things, who both yearn *and strive* for something better and finer than this world affords, have a touch of moral grandeur in their makeup that deservedly evokes admiration.

Skeptically inclined "realists" have always questioned the significance of ideals on the grounds that, being unrealizable, they are presumably pointless. But this fails to reckon properly with the realities of the situation. For while ideals are, in a way, mere fictions, they nevertheless direct and canalize our thought and action. To be sure, an ideal is not a goal we can expect to attain. But it serves to set a direction in which we can strive. Ideals are irrealities, but they are irrealities that condition the nature of the real through their influence on human thought and action. Stalin's cynical question "But how many divisions has the Pope?" betokens the Soviet *Realpolitiker* rather than the Marxist ideologue. (How many soldiers did Marx command?) It is folly to underestimate the strength of an attachment to ideals. Though in itself impracticable, an ideal can nevertheless importantly influence our praxis and serve to shape the sort of home we endeavor to make for ourselves in a difficult world.

Ideals take us beyond experience into the realm of *imagination*—outside of what we do find, or expect to find, here in this real world, into the region of wishful thinking, of utopian aspiration, of what we would fain have if only (alas!) we could. Admittedly this envisions a perfection or completion that outreaches not only what we actually have attained but what we can possibly attain in this sublunary dispensation. However, to give this up, to abandon casting those periodic wistful glances in this "transcendental" direction is to cease to be fully, genuinely, and authentically human. In following empiricists and positivists by fencing the third level of deliberation off behind "No Entry" signs, we diminish the horizons of human thought to its grave impoverishment. As is readily illustrated by examples from Galileo and Einstein, there is a valid place for thought experiments that involve idealization even in the domain of the natural sciences themselves.

The idealized level of contemplation provides a most valuable conceptual instrument. For it affords us a most useful *contrast conception* that serves to shape and condition our thought. Like the functionary in the days of imperial Rome who stood at the emperor's side to whisper intimations of mortality into his ear, so idealizations serve to remind us of the fragmentary, incomplete, and parochial nature of what we actually manage to accomplish. If the ideal level of consideration were not there for purposes of contrast, we would constantly be in danger of ascribing to the parochially proximate a degree of completeness or adequacy to which it has no just claims.

To prohibit our thought from operating at the idealized level of a global inclusiveness that transcends the reach of actual experience would create a profound impoverishment of our intellectual resources. To block off our entry into the sphere of perfection represented by the ideal level of consideration is to cut us off from a domain of thought that characterizes us as intellectually amphibious creatures who are able to operate in the realm of realities and ideals.

Such a perspective of course begs the question against the empiricist and skeptic. He wants to play safe—to have assurances that operations on the third level cannot get us into mischief. And we must concede to him that such advance assurances cannot be given. We live in a world without guarantees. All we can say is: "Try it, you'll like it—you'll find with the wisdom of hindsight that you have achieved useful results that justify the risk."

Expelled from the Garden of Eden, we are cut off from the whole sphere of completeness, perfection, comprehensiveness, and totality. We are constrained to make do with the flawed fragments of a mundane and imperfect world. But we aspire to more. Beset by a "divine discontent," we cannot but yearn for that unfettered completeness and perfection, which (as empiricists rightly emphasize) the realities of our cognitive situation cannot actually afford us. Not content with graspable satisfactions, we seek far more and press outward "beyond the limits of the possible." It is a characteristic *and worthy* feature of man to let his thought reach out toward a greater completeness and comprehensiveness than anything actually available within the mundane sphere of secured experience. *Homo sapiens* alone among earthly creatures is a being able and (occasionally) willing to work toward the realization of a condition of things that does not and perhaps even cannot exist—a state of affairs where values are fully and comprehensively embodied. He is an agent who can change and transform the world, striving to produce something that does not exist save in the mind's eye and indeed cannot actually exist at all because it calls for a greater perfection and completeness than the recalcitrant conditions of this world allow. Our commitment to this level of deliberation makes us into a creature that is something more than a rational animal—a creature that moves in the sphere of not only ideas but ideals as well.

2. *The Pragmatic Validation of Ideals*

What do ideals do for us? What useful role do they play in the scheme of things?

The answer runs something like this. Man is a rational agent. He can act and he must choose among alternative courses of action. This crucial element of choice means that our actions will be guided in the first instance by considerations of "necessity" relating to survival and physical well-being. But to some extent they can, and in an advanced condition of human development *must,* go beyond this point. And then they must be guided by necessity-transcending considerations, by man's "higher" aspirations—his yearning for a life that is not only secure and pleasant but also *meaningful* in having some element of excellence or nobility about it. Ideals are the guideposts toward these higher, excellence-oriented aspirations. As such, they motivate rather than constrain, urge rather than demand.

There are, of course, competing ideals. Aldous Huxley wrote:

> About the ideal goal of human effort there exists in our civilization and, for nearly thirty centuries, there has existed a very general agreement. From Isaiah to Karl Marx the prophets

> have spoken with one voice. In the Golden Age to which they look forward there will be liberty, peace, justice, and brotherly love. "Nation shall no more lift sword against nation"; "the free development of each will lead to the free development of all"; "the world shall be full of the knowledge of the Lord, as the waters cover the sea."[4]

Susan Stebbing took Huxley sharply to task here:

> In this judgment Mr. Huxley appears to me to be mistaken. There is not now, and there was not in 1937 when Mr. Huxley made this statement, "general agreement" with regard to "the ideal goal of human effort," even in Western Europe, not to mention Eastern Asia. The Fascist ideal has been conceived in sharpest opposition to the values which Mr. Huxley believes to be so generally acceptable, and which may be said to be characteristic of the democratic idea. The opposition is an opposition with regard to ultimate values. Fascism and democracy differ as *ideals*. The difference is emphatically not a difference merely with regard to modes of social organization; it . . . necessitates fundamental differences in the methods employed to achieve aims that are totally opposed. The ideal of Fascism is power and the glorification of the State; the ideal of democracy is the development of free and happy human beings; consequently, their most fundamental difference lies in their different conception of the worth of human beings as individuals worthy of respect.[5]

And Stebbing is quite right. Conflicting ideals are a fact of life. Different priorities can be assigned to different values, and to prize *A* over *B* is incompatible with prizing *B* over *A*.

The validation of an ideal is derivative. It does not lie in the (unrealizable) state of affairs that it contemplates—in that inherently unachievable perfection it envisions. Rather, it lies in

[4] Aldous Huxley, "Inquiry into the Nature of Ideals and the Methods Employed for Their Realization," in his *Ends and Means* (London, 1937), p. 1.

[5] L. Susan Stebbing, *Ideals and Illusions* (London, 1948), pp. 132–33.

the influence that it exerts on the lives of its human exponents through the mediation of thought. The justification and power of an ideal inhere in its capacity to energize and motivate human effort toward productive results—in short, in its practical efficacy. Ideals may involve unrealism, but this nowise annihilates their impetus or value precisely because of the practical consequences that ensue upon our adoption of them.

To be sure, one ideal can be evaluated in terms of another. But to employ our ideological commitments in appraising ideals is ultimately question begging—a matter of appraising values in terms of values. To appraise ideals in a way that avoids begging the question we must leave the domain of idealization altogether and enter into that of the realistically practical. The superiority of one ideal over another must be tested by its *practical consequences* for human well-being. "By their fruits shall ye know them." In appraising ideals we must look not to the *nature* of these ideals alone but also to their *work*. For the key role of an ideal is to serve as an instrument of decision making—a sort of navigation instrument for use in the pursuit of the good.

The impracticability of its realization is thus no insuperable obstacle to the validation of an ideal. This issue of its feasibility or infeasibility is simply beside the point, because what counts with an ideal is not the question of its *attainment* but the question of the benefits that accrue from its *pursuit*. Having and pursuing an ideal, regardless of its impracticability, can yield benefits such as a better life for ourselves and a better world for our posterity. The validation of an ideal thus lies in the pragmatic value of its pursuit. As Max Weber observed with characteristic perspicuity, even in the domain of politics, which has been called the "art of the possible," "the possible has frequently been attained only through striving for something impossible that lies beyond one's reach."[6]

But what are we to make of the fact that competing and con-

[6] "Nicht minder richtig aber ist, dass das Mögliche sehr oft nur dadurch erreicht wurde, dass man nach dem jenseits seiner Kraft liegenden Unmög-

flicting ideals are possible—that not only can different people have different ideals but one person can hold several ideals that unkind fate can force into situations of conflict and competition ("the devoted spouse" and "the successful politician," for example)?

Clearly, we have to make a good deal of this. Many things follow, including at least the following points: that life is complex and difficult; that perfection is not realizable; that lost causes may claim our allegiance and conflicts of commitment arise; that realism calls on us to harmonize our ideals even as it requires us to harmonize our other obligations in working an overall economy of values. It follows, in sum, that we must make various reciprocal adjustments and compromises. But one thing that does *not* follow is that ideals are somehow illegitimate and inappropriate.

To attain the limits of the possibilities inherent in our powers and potentialities, we must aim beyond them. And just here lies the great importance of the ideal realm. Human action cannot in general be properly understood or adequately managed without a just appreciation of the guiding ideals that lie in the background. For man's intervention in the real world sometimes is—and often should be—conditioned by his views of the ideal order in whose direction he finds it appropriate to steer the course of events.

Ideals are visionary, unrealistic, and utopian. But by viewing the world in the light of their powerful illumination, we see it all the more vividly—and critically. We understand the true nature of the real better by considering it in the light reflected from ideals, and we use this light to find our way about more satisfactorily in the real world. The power of ideals lies in the circumstance that the efficacy of our praxis can be enlarged and enhanced by looking beyond the limits of the practicable. Ideals

lichen griff." "Der Sinn der 'Wertfreiheit' in den soziologischen und ökonomischen Wissenschaften," *Logos* 7 (1917–18): 63, reprinted in *Gesammelte Aufsätze zur Wissenschaftslehre* (Tübingen, 1922), p. 476.

can render us important service when we "bring them down to earth."

To be sure, our ideals ask too much of us. We cannot attain perfection in the life of this world—not in the moral life, nor in the life of inquiry, nor in the religious life. Authentic faith, comprehensive knowledge, genuine morality are all idealizations, or destinations that we cannot actually reach. They are hyperboles that beckon us ever onward, and whose value lies in their practical utility as a motivating impetus in positive directions.

By urging us to look beyond the limits of the practicable, ideals help us to optimize the efficacy of our praxis. Their significance turns on what we *do* with them in the world—on their utility in guiding our thought and action into fruitful and rewarding directions, wholly notwithstanding their unrealistic and visionary character. Their crucial role lies in their capacity to help us to make the world a better place. There is no conflict between the demands of (valid) practice and the cultivation of (appropriate) ideals. The bearing of the practical and the ideal stand in mutually supportive cooperation.

On this account, ideals, despite their superior and splendid appearance, are actually of a subordinate status in point of justification. They are not ultimate ends but instrumental means, subservient to the ulterior values whose realization they facilitate. They are indeed important and valuable, but their worth and validity ultimately reside not in their intrinsic desirability ("wouldn't it be nice if . . .") but in their eminent utility—in their capacity to guide and to facilitate the cultivation of the values that they embody.

Such an approach to the issue of legitimating ideals has a curious aspect in its invocation of practical utility for the validation of our ideals. It maintains that the rational appropriateness of our commitment to an ideal lies in its practical utility for our dealings with the real through its capacity to encourage and facilitate our productive efforts. Such an approach does not adopt a "Platonic" view of ideals that sees them as valuable strictly in their own right. Rather, their value is seen as instrumental or pragmatic: ideals are of value not for *their own* sake but for *ours,* because of the good effects to be achieved by using them as a compass for orienting our thought and action amid the shoals and narrows of a difficult world, providing guidelines for acting so as to make one's corner of the world a more satisfying habitat for man.

This situation has its paradoxical aspect. Ideals may seem to be otherworldly, or remote from our practical concerns. But in a wider perspective, they are eminently practical, so that their legitimation is ultimately pragmatic. The imperative to ideals has that most practical of all justifications in that it facilitates the prospects of a more satisfying life. Paradoxical though it may seem, this pragmatic line is the most natural and sensible approach to the validation of ideals.

The general principle of having ideals can be defended along the following lines:

> Q: Why should people have ideals at all?
>
> A: Because this is something that is efficient and effective in implementing their pursuit of values.
>
> Q: But why should they care for the pursuit of values?
>
> A: That is simply a part of being human, and thus subject to the fundamental imperative of realizing one's potential of flourishing as the kind of creature one is.

The validity of having ideals inheres in the condition of man as an amphibian who dwells in a world of both facts and values.

Admittedly, ideals cannot be brought to actualization as such. Their very "idealized" nature prevents the arrangements they envision from constituting part of the actual furnishings of the world. But in the sphere of human endeavor we cannot properly explain and understand the reality about us without reference to motivating ideals. The contemplation of what should ideally be is inevitably bound to play an important role in the rational guidance of our actions.

The validation and legitimation of ideals accordingly lie not in their (infeasible) *applicability* but in their *utility* for directing our efforts—their productive power in providing direction and structure to our evaluative thought and pragmatic action. It is in this, their power to move the minds that move mountains, that the validation and legitimation of appropriate ideals must ultimately reside.

3. The Grandeur of Ideals

To say that the ultimate legitimation of ideals is pragmatic is not to say that they are *merely* practical—that they are somehow crass, mundane, and bereft of nobility. By no means! The mode of *justification* of ideals has effectively no bearing on their *nature* at all. Their validation may be utilitarian, but their inherent character can be transcendent. And so there need be nothing crass or mundane about our ideals as such.

With societies and nations, as with individuals, a balanced vision of the good calls for a proportionate recognition of *the domestic impetus* concerned with the well-being of people, home and hearth, stomach and pocketbook, good fellowship, rewarding work, etc. But it also calls for recognition of *the heroic impetus* concerned with acknowledging ideals, making creative achievements, playing a significant role on the world-historical stage, and doing those splendid things upon which posterity looks with admiration. Above all this latter impetus involves the winning of battles not of the battlefield but of the human mind and spirit. The absence of ideals is bound to impoverish a person or a society. Toward people or nations that have the constituents of material welfare, we may well feel envy, but our *admiration* and *respect* could never be won on this ground alone. Excellence must come into it. And in this excellence-connected domain we leave issues of utility behind and enter another sphere—that of human ideals relating to man's higher and nobler aspirations.

Homo sapiens is a rational animal. The fact that we are animals squarely emplaces us within the order of nature. But the fact that we are rational exempts us from an absolute rule by external forces. It means that our nature is not wholly *given*, that we are able to contribute in at least some degree toward making ourselves into the sort of creatures we are. A rational creature is inevitably one that has some capacity to let its idealized vision of what it should be determine what it actually is. It is in this sense that an involvement with ideals is an essential aspect of the human condition.

4. *Conclusion*

Their fictional nature does not destroy the usefulness of ideals. To be sure, we do not—should not—expect to bring ideals to realization. Yet an ideal is like the Holy Grail of medieval romance: it impels us onward in the journey and gives meaning and direction to our efforts. Rewards of dignity and worth lie in these efforts themselves, irrespective of the question of actual attainment. When appraising a person's life, the question "What did he endeavor?" is as relevant as the question "What did he achieve?"

The objects at issue in our ideals are not parts of the world's furniture. Like utopias and mythic heroes (or the real-world heroes we redesign in their image by remaking these people into something that never was), ideals are "larger than life." The states of affairs at issue with ideals do not and cannot exist as such. Look about us where we will, we shall not find them actualized. The directive impetus that they give us generally goes under the name of "inspiration." They call to us to bend our efforts toward certain unattainable goals. Yet, though fictions, they are eminently *practical* fictions. They find their utility not in application to the things of this world but in their bearing upon the thoughts that govern our actions within it. They are not *things* as such but *thought instrumentalities* that orient and direct our praxis in the direction of realizing a greater good.

Yet ideals, though instruments of thought, are not mere myths. For there is nothing false or fictional about ideals as such—only about the idea of their embodiment in concrete reality. Their pursuit is something that can be perfectly real—and eminently productive. (And it is at this pragmatic level that the legitimation of an ideal must ultimately be sought.)

Still, given the inherent unrealizability of what is at issue, are ideals not indelibly irrational?

Here, as elsewhere, we must reckon with the standard gap between aspiration and attainment. In the practical sphere—for example, in craftsmanship or the cultivation of our health—we may *strive* for perfection, but we cannot ever claim to *attain* it. Moreover, the situation in inquiry is exactly parallel, as is that in morality or in statesmanship. The cognitive ideal of perfected science stands on the same level as the moral ideal of a perfect agent or the political ideal of a perfect state. The value of such unrealizable ideals lies not in the (unavailable) benefits of attainment but in the benefits that accrue from pursuit. The view that it is rational to pursue an aim only if we are in a position to achieve its attainment or approximation is simply mistaken. As we have seen, an unattainable end can be perfectly valid (and entirely rational) if the indirect benefits of its pursuit are sufficient—if in striving after it, we realize relevant advantages to a substantial degree. An unattainable ideal can be enormously productive.

The issue of justifying the adoption of unattainable ideals thus brings us back to the starting point of these deliberations—the defense of the appropriateness of fighting for lost causes. Optimal results are often attainable only by trying for too much—by reaching beyond the limits of the possible. Man is a dual citizen of the realms of reality and possibility. He must live and labor *in* the one but *toward* the other. The person whose wagon is not hitched to some star or other is not a full-formed human being; he is less than he can and should be.

It seems particularly incongruous to condemn the pursuit of ideals as contrary to *rationality*. For one thing, rationality is a matter of the intelligent pursuit of appropriate ends, and ideals form part of the framework with reference to which our determinations of appropriateness proceed. No less relevant, however, is the fact that a good case can be made for holding that complete rationality is itself something unrealizable, given the enormously comprehensive nature of what is demanded (for example, by recourse to the principle of total evidence for rationally constituted belief and action). Neither in matters of thought nor in matters of action can we ever succeed in being totally and completely rational; we have to recognize that perfect rationality is itself an unattainable ideal. And we must be realistic about the extent to which we can implement this ideal amid the harsh realities of a difficult world. Yet even though total rationality is unattainable, its pursuit is nevertheless perfectly rational because of the great benefits that it palpably engenders. It is thus ironic that the thoroughgoing rationality in whose name the adoption of unattainable ends is sometimes condemned itself represents an unattainable ideal whose pursuit is rationally defensible only by pragmatically oriented arguments of the general sort considered here.

To be sure, this practicalistic sort of validation of ideals leaves untouched the issue of *which* particular values are to prevail. The approach is a general one and thus does not address the justification of particular ideals. It indicates the importance of having some ideals or other, leaving the issue of specific commitments aside. For addressing *this* issue requires more than an abstract analysis of the nature and function of ideals; it calls for articulating and defending a concrete philosophy of life. And this, of course, is an issue beyond the range of our present deliberations.

But the fact remains that it is important—and crucially so—for a person to have guiding ideals. A life without ideals need not be a life without purpose, but it will be a life without purposes of a sort in which one can appropriately take reflective satisfaction. The person for whom values matter so little that he has no ideals is condemned to wander through life disoriented, without guiding beacons to furnish that sense of direction that gives meaning and point to the whole enterprise. Someone who lacks ideals suffers an impoverishment of spirit for which no other resources can adequately compensate.

Index of Names

Subject Index

Designer:	Janet Wood
Compositor:	Graphic Composition
Text:	11/13 Sabon
Display:	Sabon
Printer:	Edwards Brothers
Binder:	Edwards Brothers